The Highly Sensitive Empath

How To Stop Emotional Overload, Find Your Sense Of Self, And Thrive In An Overwhelming World

Theresa Evans

Table Of Contents:

Introduction

Have you ever been called too sensitive? Do people ask you to toughen up and not be over-sensitive? Do you feel extremely drained when you are out in public? Does it make you feel anxious when you are around certain people? Do you experience an undeniable urge to fix the problems of others? Do you feel like you can help those who are in need? If yes, then it is quite likely that you are an empath.

There was a point in my life when everything seemed to be going wrong. It felt like I was completely out of control, and there was nothing I could do to make things better for myself. I wasn't doing well at work, and this was one of the reasons why I couldn't sleep at night. It also meant that I was getting more and more stressed about my work. All these factors kept fueling each other, and I was stuck in a vicious cycle of stress and anxiety from which I couldn't escape. My anxiety and stress became so bad that I couldn't even stomach the food I ate at work. However, once I was in the safety of my own living room, I would feel better.

This was also the time in my life when I was going through an "I am not sensitive" phase. I tried quite hard to maintain this façade and even took pride in the fact that nothing bothered me. I was ignoring my true feelings and emotions so much that I started to get disconnected from my true self. I no longer understood what was going on within me. Frankly, I was operating at such an elevated level of physical stress, which is quite impossible for a highly sensitive person to sustain. Miraculously, I managed to survive. I felt like I hit the absolute rock bottom in life. This was when I realized it was time for a one-on-one session with myself. It was around the same time I was studying psychology. I understood where I was going wrong. After a little introspection, I realized that I wasn't following the advice I kept reading about- I failed to accept myself.

When you grow up in a society that keeps telling you to stop being "oversensitive," you reach a stage where you stop feeling anything. I reached this stage, and this is where I went wrong. If you feel like this, then this is because you are suppressing your empathy. Don't be afraid to accept your emotions and feelings. Once I embraced my empathic abilities, and true self, I started to feel better. I finally regained control of my life and realized that being an empath was a superpower with which I was blessed. Yes, it makes me different from others, but I love that I am unique and not like everyone else. Now that I understand my empathic abilities, I have seen a positive change in my life.

This experience made me want to help others like me. If you feel like you are struggling with your emotions and are unable to understand your empathic abilities, then I am here for you. You are not alone, and there are plenty of people like us across the globe. However, if you do want to change, then you must take action immediately. Realize that the power to turn your life around and regulate your emotions lies in your hands. In this book, I will share with you all the knowledge I gained through my experiences as an empath and extensive research I did about empaths. If you're willing to put in the necessary effort, time, and self-love, you can turn your life around. Learn to be patient with yourself and extend the same compassion towards yourself as you do towards others.

This is the perfect book not just for empaths, but also for all those people who are in different stages of empathy. If you want to figure yourself out and learn to deal with your emotions, then this book holds all the solutions you seek. In this book, you will learn about everything related to leading life as an empath. It all starts with a simple self-test questionnaire to determine your level of empathy. After this, you will learn about understanding your gift and assessing your empathic abilities. Once you do this, it is time to determine the type of an empath you are.

You will learn about neuroscience, which fuels empathy, how you can deal with different relationships, and deal with your professional life as an empath. Apart from these topics, you will also learn about how you can establish stronger and better bonds with others. All the chapters in this book are accompanied by different exercises you can practice to improve your empathic abilities. Carefully go through the information in this book, along with the various exercises, to get a better understanding of yourself and your empathic skills.

So, if you're ready to get started, then there is no time like the present to get started!

Chapter 1: Self-Test- Are You A Highly Sensitive Empath

Did you ever meet someone who seemed to be able to understand all your thoughts and feelings? Are you that person? If yes, then you are probably an empath. So, what does it mean to be an empath? Before determining whether you are an empath or not, it is essential to understand what empathy means.

The ability to resonate with, understand, and read others is known as empathy. Empathy can be voluntary as well as involuntary. If a person is a natural empath, then the abilities, as mentioned earlier, are almost always automatic. Empaths are highly sensitive, and they tend to experience a high degree of understanding and compassion towards others. This intense sense of empathy given off by empaths tends to create the effect of a tuning fork, which essentially makes them feel and experience the feelings or emotions of those around them. Only a few empaths are actually aware of this gift they process, and most of them merely write it off by assuming that they are just too sensitive.

I like to think of empaths as artists, dreamers, natural healers, and highly creative individuals. The artistic community is usually filled with empaths. Their talents, as well as their interests, are quite varied and broad. They come from different walks of life and are present everywhere. You might be an empath yourself, or you might know an empath. There is no specific label that defines them, and anyone can be an empath. I believe that empaths are the listeners of life.

If you possess the ability to understand someone else's thoughts, as well as feelings, from their perspective instead of your own perspective, then you possess the gift of empathy. Even if you don't have any similar experiences like the people around you, you can still understand them. There are a couple of core values that all empaths share like an instinct to nurture, establish deep and meaningful relationships, and non-judgment. These values are present in all empaths.

An empath is not just affected by the feelings, energies, and emotions of others, but also their thoughts and actions. All empaths are blessed with an innate ability to understand all those they come across in life. Empaths can quickly understand the underlying motivations for the actions, intentions, and desires of those they cross paths within their lives. Simply put, I think empaths are consciously as well as unconsciously capable of being attuned with those around them while understanding them emotionally.

As an empath, you are extremely sensitive and aware of the emotions and energies of others. You might even assume the emotions of others are your own. It might be rather challenging if you don't have any boundaries to restrict this sharing of energy. If you aren't careful, you might end up feeling quite overwhelmed because of all these emotions.

Do you think you are an empath? Are you sensitive to different smells, light, and sound? Do you feel restless when you don't get some alone time to destress? Can you experience what others experience? Does your heart go out to someone who seems rather sad? Do you think you can understand others regardless of how well they are able to convey their feelings? If yes, then you are probably an empath.

Empath Self-Assessment

Carefully go through the different question is given in this section and answer them honestly. Take all the time you require while answering them. When in doubt, you can always ask for the help of your loved ones. However, I don't think you will need any extra help to answer these questions. Merely listen to your gut, and you will soon have your answers. So, let us get started.

1. Have you ever been labeled as being shy, introverted, or even overly sensitive?
2. Do you feel overwhelmed or anxious for no reason, and does this happen regularly?
3. Do you feel like you just don't fit in and that you are quite different from others?
4. Do you ever feel mentally tired and drained out after spending time in public?
5. Do you feel better when you spend time by yourself, and does it help revive your energy levels?
6. Does getting into arguments or shouting matches make you physically sick?
7. Do different odors, or even noises make you feel overstimulated?
8. Do you get tired when you spend too much time with those who talk nonstop?
9. Do you have any chemical sensitivity or a low tolerance towards scratchy clothes?

10. Do you usually travel by yourself so that you're free to leave whenever you want to?

11. Do you tend to isolate yourself socially?

12. Do intimate relationships scare you and make you feel like you're being suffocated?

13. Do you get startled rather easily?

14. Do you binge eat to cope with anxiety or stress?

15. Do you have any intense reactions towards medications or even caffeine?

16. Is your pain threshold quite low?

17. Do you prefer concentrating on one task at a time?

18. Do you like to multitask?

19. Does multitask stress you out or induce anxiety?

20. Do you tend to absorb the emotions and feelings of those around you?

21. If you have been around people who keep sucking out your energy, does it take you a long time to recharge your batteries?

22. Do you feel better when you spend time in nature?

23. Do you prefer small gatherings and one-on-one conversations?

24. Do you prefer the quaint countryside to the hustle-bustle of city life?

25. Do you tend to understand how others feel even if they're trying to hide it?

26. Do you try to avoid conflict because you don't want to hurt the feelings of others or make them feel embarrassed?

27. Do you ever unconsciously mimic the mannerisms of those you converse with?

28. Does injustice draw you in, and do you start thinking about ways to alleviate all the suffering you see?

29. Do you ever feel extremely disturbed whenever you make a social blunder?

30. Do you feel uncomfortable when you watch anything violent on television and movies?

31. Do you feel happy when you watch romantic comedies or any happy movies?

32. Do you ever experience any protective feelings towards complete strangers and not just the ones you love?

33. Do others seek your advice when they are in trouble?

Calculate your results

You would be a partial empath if your answers were yes to at least 6 to 8 questions in this section. If your answer is no to all of these questions, then you possess no empathy whatsoever. If that's the case, then I strongly urge you to work on cultivating empathy immediately. If your answer was yes to about 9 to 14 questions, then you possess a moderate degree of empathy. You would have strong empathic tendencies if your answers were yes for about 18 questions. If your answer was yes to more than 18 questions, then you are a full-blown empath. Regardless of your answers, the different strategies, along with the helpful information given in this book, will enable you to master your empathic abilities.

Empath and Being Empathetic

Being empathetic and being an empath might sound like the same thing, but there is a slight difference between the two. When you are empathetic, your heart might go out to someone else whenever you see their suffering or pain. However, if you are an empath, you tend to actually experience what the other person is feeling as if it was radiating from your own body.

A specialized group of cells known as the mirror neuron system is present in all human beings, and it is responsible for generating feelings of compassion. In an empath, this system is rather hyperactive, and it works on overdrive all the time. Because of all this, empaths can easily absorb the energies given off by others into their own bodies and experience it as if it was generated in their own system. This means empaths can absorb both positive as well as negative emotions easily. At times, it might even become difficult for you to determine whether the emotion you're experiencing is your own or borrowed.

There are various types of sensitivities that empaths can experience. For instance, physical empaths are attuned towards the physical symptoms or needs of others, and they tend to absorb the same into their own bodies. On the other hand, emotional empaths tend to pick up on the emotions and feelings of those around them. Emotional empaths are like sponges that soak up everything around them.

Being empathic has various benefits like compassion, creativity, intuition, and the ability to form strong bonds with others. However, living in this heightened state of sensitivity can become quite challenging. Empaths can become easily overwhelmed, overstimulated, and even extremely drained out because of all the stress or negativity they absorb from others. It's not just about absorbing the emotions of others, but empaths also give away their positive energies in this process.

If an individual isn't aware of his empathic abilities, then even daily interactions can become increasingly intolerable and cause extreme levels of stress. Those who are not aware of their empathic abilities might unconsciously turn to alcohol, drugs, or even food to quiet their hyperactive emotions. If you have answered all the questions in the questionnaire, and have calculated your results, you will have your answer about whether you are an empath or not.

I like to think of empaths as the much-needed medicine in this chaotic and turbulent world in which we live. Their compassion, coupled with their innate ability to understand and nurture others, can have a positive effect on humanity. Once you accept the fact that you're an empath and start identifying your unique talents, you can easily enrich your life. Not just this, but you can also help heal others and enrich their lives along the way. The one skill you must learn is to control your sensitivities and adopt specific strategies that prevent an overload of emotions. You will learn about all this in the subsequent chapters.

Traits of Empaths

Now that you have determined your level of empathy, we can move on to the next step. Carefully go through the list of traits discussed in this section to get a better understanding of what it means to be an empath.

Empaths are extremely sensitive and are capable of determining the slightest changes in other's energies. This sensitivity includes physical sensations along with interpersonal aspects.

Usually, empaths have a good understanding of their emotions and feelings. So, they are quite intuitive. Therefore, they are adept at sensing things long before others start taking note of it. Their intuition often helps them avoid toxic people.

Most empaths are usually introverted. It does not mean that all introverts are empaths. At the same time, it doesn't mean that all empaths are introverts. Introversion is a common trait among empaths. Interacting with large groups is somewhat overwhelming for empaths, and this is the reason why they like spending time away from crowds.

Empaths are quite selfless, almost to a fault. An egotist never thinks about anyone else's needs except his own. Empaths, on the other hand, will always put others' needs above their own. If you do this, then this is one aspect you must work on fixing. You must never ignore your own needs merely to satisfy someone else's wants.

Since empaths understand what others are feeling, it makes it easier for them to connect with others.

Empaths are quite forgiving. Their ability to forgive often stems from the fact that they usually see themselves in others. Perhaps, this is the reason why they're able to understand the problems, as well as the challenges, that others face. Apart from this, there are also aware of all the emotional baggage that others carry. For this reason, they can be quite forgiving.

One unique ability all empaths possess is to see through the lies and deceptive ways of others. Since empaths are intuitive, they can see the true intentions of all those people they come across in life.

Empaths are natural healers, and they are all born with an inherent desire to fix others' problems and make this world more livable. Another interesting characteristic of all empaths is that there are quite curious.

They are usually looking for answers and love asking thought-provoking questions. At the same time, they can be quite absent-minded too. Typically, they are often overwhelmed by the different emotions they come across that they forget about their own feelings. This means that they tend to lose touch with reality and often get lost in all these emotions they experience.

Not a lot of people are capable of accepting their faults or taking responsibility for their actions. However, this is one thing all empaths are really good at. Empaths never try to shift the responsibility onto others. Playing the blame game is not something an empath would want to do. Since they are good at taking responsibility for their actions, they are often used as patsies by manipulative individuals.

Empaths are quite creative. They love indulging in activities that allow them to exploit the full extent of their creativity and imagination. This also means that they are daydreamers. They usually find it difficult to concentrate on a specific task, and multitasking is not their strong suit.

An empath can never fully relax when others are around. This is because an empath is continuously experiencing whatever the other person is feeling, so it becomes quite difficult to relax. This is one of the reasons why empaths prefer being on their own. Empaths tend to thrive when they are around happy and vibrant people. No one likes being around selfish, mean, and dull individuals; an empath especially dislikes it with great fervor.

Empaths are quite compassionate. Their compassion allows them to be extremely tolerant of insecurities, weaknesses, or any flaws that others have. They usually see themselves in others, and this is the reason why they are very kind to others.

Empaths often struggle to understand the source of the emotions they experience. Since they keep absorbing the emotions and feelings of all those people around them, it becomes difficult to know whether the feelings they're experiencing are their own or someone else's. This is also a source of confusion for them.

Empaths understand emotions and emotional baggage better than anyone else. This is one of the reasons why some people tend to think of empaths as a dumping ground for emotional baggage.

Another interesting characteristic of an empath is that they are quite connected to nature. Animals, plants, and even natural landscapes are quite sacred to empaths. In fact, most empaths feel better after they spend some time in nature instead of crowded places.

Empaths find it quite challenging to say no to others. Whenever they see pain or suffering, they try to fix this situation. This means, if someone asks something of them, they are usually unable to say no or refuse the requests posed.

Chapter 2: Understanding Your Gift

Your Capabilities

Empaths are highly sensitive, and it means that they can quickly feel and absorb the emotions along with any physical symptoms others experience. Their intuition usually helps them navigate the intricacies of the real world, and this makes it difficult to rationalize all that they feel. Not just as a psychologist, but also as a fellow empath, I fully understand all the challenges associated with being highly sensitive. When confronted with highly charged situations and overwhelming emotions, empaths can experience various physiological symptoms that go beyond the diagnosis of traditional medicine. From panic attacks to chronic depression and fatigue, these physiological symptoms are all because of dealing with overwhelming emotions, which are not necessarily your own.

That said, the benefits of being an empath, outweigh all the possible accompanying challenges. If you want to learn to regain control of your life and regulate your feelings, then the first step is to acknowledge the fact that you are an empath. In this section, you will learn about the capabilities of an empath.

High level of sensitivity

Empaths exhibit a high degree of sensitivity and are naturally nurturing. They are good listeners and have a giving nature. When you look at a group of friends, an empath would be that one friend who always stands by others through thick and thin. If you are that friend, then kudos to you. It isn't easy to be there for everyone. Since you can easily understand what others are feeling and empathize with them, people will naturally turn to you for advice. Whenever someone is feeling a little low on energy, they will seek you. The energy radiated by empaths is almost magnetic, especially to those who are running low on energy.

Have you ever been told that you are too sensitive or a little too touchy? Well, I know I've been told this repeatedly growing up and even in my adulthood. I used to shy away from my empathy. Only when I realized that I was an empath did everything finally make sense to me. The way empaths process and experience emotions is quite different from others. Empaths not only have to deal with what they feel, but they also have to deal with the energy that comes with the way others deal with emotions. It isn't always easy to handle all this. If you have been told to toughen up, that's a good piece of advice. However, toughening up doesn't mean ignoring your emotions or blocking whatever you feel. God knows I tried all this, but it doesn't work. Before you can toughen up, you must learn to understand and accept your feelings.

Then you must work on distinguishing these feelings from those of others around you.

Absorbing others' emotions

Since you are quite sensitive to the moods of others, everything you feel tends to be on the extreme sides of the spectrum. All the negativity, like anger or anxiety, which stems from others, is rather tiring and training. On the other hand, when you're surrounded by piece, positivity, and love, you tend to thrive. You can absorb others' emotions, both good as well as bad. It merely depends on you to determine what or whom you let in.

Introverted nature

Being in a crowded situation or around too many people all the time is draining for an empath. If you take a moment and think about it, it will make perfect sense to you. If you are too many people, it means you're around too many emotions. All these emotions are continually invading your personal space. Therefore, it is not surprising that a lot of empaths prefer being on their own. Even if you were an extrovert, you would certainly like to limit your social interactions. Regardless of how much fun you have when others are around, you probably enjoy retreating to a quiet space to recharge your batteries.

Intuitive

As I mentioned, empaths tend to navigate the world and experience it through their intuitive abilities. As an empath, I strongly suggest that you work on developing your intuition. Start listening to what your gut tells you about people as well as situations. If something feels wrong to you, then it probably is. Start listening to your gut and avoid everything that feels wrong. By doing this, you can effectively avoid interacting with toxic people and energy vampires. Instead of unnecessarily squandering your energy, you can work on developing positive relationships with people who help and nourish you.

Alone time

What happens when you don't charge your phone for two days in a row? Obviously, the battery drains out. Likewise, even your energy starts to drain out when you don't give yourself some alone time. Spend some time by yourself and solitude, and you will feel better. Even a brief escape from a crowded room is quite helpful. It is okay to need some alone time, and in fact, it is quite good for your overall wellbeing.

Intimate relationships

Spending too much time around anyone can be draining for an empath. This means intimate relationships become rather tricky for empaths. If you are in close quarters with another person all the time, it becomes difficult to ignore their energy fields. This is one of the reasons why empaths don't prefer intimate relationships. I used to be scared of long-term relationships because I was worried about losing my identity in the relationship. I was worried that all the emotions I would experience wouldn't be my own. And that there would always be someone else sharing my personal space. Then I realized that this isn't how it has to be. By redefining the rules of a traditional relationship, I found success. Now, I know that I can spend time with my loved ones while taking care of myself. I don't have to compromise on self-care and my alone time. Likewise, neither do you.

Confusion

A lot of people tend to behave inconsistently. They're almost like chameleons that regularly change their colors. A person might behave differently in different circumstances, and this is quite normal. However, when you're around people who constantly keep changing their behavior and personality, it becomes quite confusing for you. All this is because of your empathic nature. Since you can absorb what others are feeling, all changing behaviors and inconsistencies can become overwhelming for you. This, in turn, can make it seem like a burden to you.

Connect the dots

As an empath, you not only understand what the other person is going through but also the reason they are going through it. Once you know the reason for their behavior, it becomes easier to figure things out. Essentially, it helps make it easier for you to connect the dots and gain some helpful insights about others. It also means you become quite good at spotting deception.

Challenges

There are certainly a couple of problems you need to overcome because of your empathic abilities. In this section, you'll learn about the daily challenges faced by empaths.

Improve your energetic literacy

You must work on improving your energetic literacy. Energetic literacy essentially refers to a concept that helps you understand nature or along with the role of energy in the real world. Once you understand this concept, you must start using it to solve any obstacles or challenges that come along your way. If you want to be energy literate, then you must be able to do the following.

- Understand the way energy flows.
- Understand the use of energy, its purpose, and the source of energy.
- Easily assess the credibility of information associated with this energy.

- Learn to communicate and use the energy for meaningful purposes.
- Ability to make informed decisions about using this energy based on the analysis of the consequences involved.

Learn to read your energy signature

Everything in this universe is made of energy, and everything vibrates at a different frequency. For instance, by setting the radio station to a specific channel, you can listen to a particular kind of music. If you change the channel, the music will change. Every radio station works at a specific frequency and offers specific information. Different listeners are attracted to different frequencies that match their personal preferences. Likewise, the energy that you keep giving out attracts different people to you. If you weren't careful, you might end up attracting toxic people and energy vampires. Therefore, it is quintessential to understand your energy signature. You must become aware of yourself, your feelings, and the energy you give out. I suggest that you start treating the energy present within you as something sacred. It isn't to be shared with everyone, and you must be selective about those you share it with and those you let in. If you are careful, you merely burn yourself out or fall prey to an emotional predator.

Manage afflictions

You must learn to manage afflictions because of the high degree of sensitivity you possess. If you want to make your life easier and replenish your energy, then you must learn to strike a balance. If you are careful, you'll end up getting hot. To prevent this, you must work on setting certain boundaries for yourself. You must typically set these boundaries and also stick to them. Don't ever try to change yourself to accommodate others. If you keep changing yourself and try fulfilling any unreasonable demands that others have, you will merely end up hurting your own energy. In the long run, it will take a toll on your body, mind, and soul. If you are stuck in a toxic relationship, then it is time to end it. Make a list of all the things, which drain you of your positive energy and maintain your distance from them. Don't give in to any addictions to support the toxicity in your life or the stress you feel. Empaths can get easily addicted to different things because of their sensitive nature. Once you create a dependency, it becomes rather difficult to break free of it.

Listen to intuition

You must work on listening to your gut feeling. Your intuition is there for a reason, and it is high time that you start listening to it. As mentioned earlier, your intuition allows you to navigate the intricacies of life. The only way to develop your intuition and strengthen your gut feeling is by developing your self-esteem and self-confidence. Once you are confident about yourself, your thoughts, and feelings, it becomes easier to trust the little voice in your head.

Opportunities

There are different opportunities available to you because of your empathic abilities. These skills certainly make you different from those around you. Instead of worrying that you are different from others, try to think of yourself as being unique. I know there might have been times when your empathic abilities make you feel frustrated, tired, drained out, and even confused for no apparent reason. There are some drawbacks to being an empath, but with a little conscious effort, you can quickly turn these drawbacks to work for you. If you want to lead your life to the fullest, then you must learn to appreciate yourself and the empathy you possess. I have come across people who feel lost in this chaotic world because of their empathic side. I am going to give you the same advice I gave them- understand your gift, accept it, and cherish it. Once you do this, you can lead the kind of life you always desired.

Empathy is a skill only a few have

Empathy is a superpower that only a few possess. So, you can either think of yourself as being weird or as a superhero. It is entirely up to you the way you want to interpret this. If you think of it as a superpower, you will feel better about yourself and will be more comfortable in your skin. There are so many people who struggle to understand those around them. This is something about which you never have to worry. As an empath, you will quickly know what others are thinking. You don't have to worry about being others lying to you! Just trust your gut, and it will guide you through life. Once you open your mind to all the possibilities offered by your empathic abilities, you would become a force to be reckoned.

Potential to help others

When you know what others are thinking and feeling, it becomes easier to help them. People often struggle to express themselves. Even when they are in a world of misery, they often put up a façade for the world. We have all been conditioned by society to believe that certain emotions aren't desirable and expressing them is not proper. Because you are an empath, you can discern what others are feeling even if they haven't expressed it. Once you understand how to process your emotions and feelings and start distinguishing it from those of others around you, you can control your empathic abilities. This puts you in a position to help others.

First aid person for people's minds and hearts

Are you the first person your friends or loved ones turn to whenever they are in trouble? Do your friends come to you whenever they feel sad? Are you their agony aunt? Well, this is because of your empathic abilities. Even if they don't know that you are an empath, your energy naturally draws them to you. This is one of the most wonderful things about being an empath. People will be at their most vulnerable when they come to you for help. Your energy is almost like a band-aid for any troubles they have. However, you must learn to manage other's energy that enters your personal field of energy. If you leave it unregulated, you will quickly burn yourself out.

Natural born healers

Since you naturally know what others want or what is bothering them, you can help them. Most empaths are natural healers. Practicing some form of healing, whether conventional or even alternative medicine, is one of the common professions that empaths usually choose. I used my empathic abilities and channeled it toward a career in psychology. You can put your skills to good use, provided you know what to do with them. You will be able to see blockages in the energy fields of those around you or any undesirable changes in their energy levels. This will help you identify any problems allowing you will to help others.

Importance grounding

Well, you can certainly help a lot of people with your empathic abilities. That being said, you must take care of your personal energy field too. You can't allow others to trample over you or take any undue advantage of your helpful nature. You must first take care of yourself before you attempt to help others. Did you ever go through the safety manuals place in aircraft? What is the instruction for using oxygen masks? The instruction is quite simple- always place your mask on first before you help others. Likewise, I appreciate the fact that you want to help others, but if you don't take care of yourself, you will not be of much help. How can you help others when you are running on fumes? Therefore, you must stay grounded and in sync with your reality. Learn to take stock of your energy levels, stay away from toxic people and environment, and do things that make you happy. When you are happy, your energy vibrates at high levels, and you will be better equipped to help others. You will learn more about all this in the subsequent chapters.

The mission is to help not to use skills to weird out other people

This might sound like a rather obvious piece of advice, but don't use your gift to make others feel uncomfortable or weird. Your role as an empath is to help others and bring about a sense of peace and harmony to this chaotic world in which we live. Don't use your skills to weird out others, and instead, try to be as helpful as you can. However, don't help others at your expense. Always tend to yourself before you lend a helping hand.

Empath vs. Highly Sensitive Person

Empaths are highly attuned to the feelings of those around them. It would be fair to call them highly sensitive. However, an empath is different from a highly sensitive person (HSP). These words are often used synonymously, but they aren't. The nervous systems of HSP are quite sensitive to the energies of those present around them. Being present in a highly stimulating environment can be rather overwhelming for an HSP. All empaths also exhibit this kind of sensitivity. So, are you wondering what the difference is? Well, the difference between these two personality types lies in their ability to feel and perceive other's feelings. Empaths tend to experience the emotions and feeling quite literally, or at times, even the physical state of those around them.

Empathy is present in all humans but to varying degrees. Some are incapable of feeling any empathy whatsoever like sociopaths. If you get to know that your best friend lost her spouse, how would an average human being react? The normal, acceptable, and expected reaction in such situations is to offer condolences. Regardless of whether others can experience her grief or not, they will offer their sympathy and condolences. As an empath, you will be able to feel her grief as if it was your own loss. You not only feel bad for her but also experience her sorrow. Others might be able to comprehend her loss, but they cannot fully understand it, but you can. Likewise, if your partner has a migraine, then chances are that you will also experience a headache when you are around your partner.

Now, let us talk about an HSP. A highly sensitive person might feel overwhelmed at the thought of losing their partner. This reaction is all associated with their extremely sensitive nervous system.

However, this is where the similarities end. An HSP might even use his friend's tragic loss and make it all about himself. In fact, I will not be surprised if the HSP starts to unravel and start feeling like he is stuck in a hopeless world sans any good. At this point, he isn't trying to help his friend the way an empath would; instead, his primary focus is on himself and his thoughts. The HSP might also use his friend's personal tragedy as an excuse for any apparent pain he experiences.

To be fair, it wouldn't be right to state that all highly sensitive individuals would misappropriate their emotions. There are always exceptions to certain rules. The energy in the surrounding environment can be a trigger for an HSP. Once their response is triggered, they will become the focal point, and no one else matters. An empath can feel whatever others feel; an HSP cannot. The common trait between these two personality types is that dealing with emotions, especially big emotions are tricky for them.

HSP is always reactive to the energy around them, and they tend to project their sensitivity onto others. An HSP might also conclude that others are feeling whatever he is feeling. He fails to understand that he is projecting and is often ruled by his emotional state. HSP might be completely unaware of the fact that he has made himself the focal point, even if the issue doesn't concern him.

Highly sensitive people aren't usually good at reading and understanding the emotions of those around them. They can understand when there is a change in the energy around them, but they don't understand the cause of such change. They are often so caught up in their own narrative that they seldom have time to think about other's perspectives. They are sensitive as well as reactive, but not in a way that's always desirable.

Empaths can feel and experience what others do, understand where others are coming from, and why they do what they do. A highly sensitive person is merely sensitive to the energy of those around him. Empaths will not try to make themselves the focal point in any scenario, but HSP will not mind doing so.

Therefore, it is safe to say that all empaths are highly sensitive. However, all highly sensitive people don't necessarily have to be empaths. In fact, narcissists and sociopaths are highly sensitive individuals. They can pick on the feelings and emotions of their victims. Once they identify what their victim feels, they target them. An empath would never do this. Empath's first response would be to help others, whereas, the first response of a highly sensitive person might be self-protection.

Exercises to Calibrate Yourself

Visual

One of the downsides of being an empath is that you are in constant touch with external energies.

Unless you are consciously paying attention to those you come in contact with and try to block it out, you cannot ignore these energies. Because of this constant contact, it is quite likely that you will start to lose touch with your self-identity. To prevent this, you must practice visualization exercises. It is time to create a dream board for yourself. You are essentially building a collage of your identity. This board can include pictures of all those you love, places you enjoy or want to visit, things that make you happy or relaxed, and pictures you relate to. Once you make this board, place it such that you can glance at it daily.

Auditive

Music is one of the most therapeutic forms of relaxation. Music can instantly lift your spirits and feel you pumped up. This is one of the reasons why they blare pumped up and energetic music at gyms and relaxing music in restaurants. The power of music can never be overlooked. Make a list of all your favorite songs and listen to them on your way to work, whenever you take a break or are bored. You can also listen to your playlist as you go about doing other routine tasks like cleaning the house or even taking a shower. Whenever you need to relax or let go of any negative energies, listen to your favorite songs. In fact, I think it is a good idea to sing along. Sing your heart out, even if you aren't a good singer. It is quite unlikely that you will stay sad while singing the lyrics of a peppy, upbeat number!

Grounding technique

Learning to stay grounded is quite important for every human being, but it is doubly important if you are an empath. It is quite easy to get bogged down because of all the external energies you keep absorbing. Simple grounding exercises will help you deal with the daily stresses of life as an empath. Along with this, they enable you to live in the moment, without worrying about things you cannot control, like the past and the future. Always end your day with a grounding exercise. One technique that helped me a lot is journalizing. Before I go to sleep at night, I spend a couple of minutes and make a list of all the different things that make me feel grateful. I make a note of ten things I enjoyed about my day and am happy. It can be something as simple as the free ice cream I got at the cafeteria or even the roses blooming on the sidewalk. This helps me feel good about myself and the reality of life. Along with grounding, journalizing also helps shift your focus so that you start to become more appreciative of the world and all its beauty. Whenever I feel low on energy, I go through my gratitude journal, and I instantly feel better. Regardless of how tired you feel at night, don't forget to write your daily journal entry.

Chapter 3: Assessing Your Empathic Abilities And Type

Abilities of an Empath

Empaths are like real-life superheroes. I know I feel better about my empathic abilities whenever I think of myself as a superhero who is helping others. Our ability to sense what others need, how they feel, and understand their emotions makes us quite different from others. Being an empath is a wonderful gift, and here are the different abilities with which all empaths are blessed.

Vision

When you fully tap into your empathic abilities, you will realize that you can easily spot the symbolism in any scenario. All empaths are blessed with the ability to understand what is happening not just in their bodies, but in those around them along with the situation they are in.

This pretty much gives a bird's eye view of any scenario they are earned. So, you are equipped with the ability to disengage from any situation and carefully look at any underlying issue that needs to be addressed. Most human beings often cannot see beyond what is superficially visible. However, empaths can look past this and try to understand the deeper meaning in any situation.

Empaths are capable of understanding the true feelings of those around them. Even if others try to mask their emotions, they seldom succeed while dealing with empaths. Once you take full responsibility for your gifts and know how to use them, you can start bringing about much-needed harmony in this world. This same power can also make you feel a little vulnerable from time to time. However, once you understand how to regulate your empathic abilities and start using it with discernment, it becomes a rather powerful tool. If you feel like others are often taking advantage of you or are walking all over you, it is time to take a stand for yourself. You can do this by working on improving your empathic skills.

Intuition

Did you ever hear a tiny voice in your head when you are making a mistake? Do you ever meet someone and do tiny alarm bells start ringing in your head? Do you feel nervousness in the pit of your stomach whenever you're about to do something you probably know is not right? If yes, then all these instances are your intuition trying to talk to you. Your intuition is the tiny voice in your head that guides you and tells you whenever you make a mistake. All humans have intuition, but an empath's intuitive ability is unlike anyone else's.

There are seven main chakras in the body, and the Manipura chakra (solar plexus chakra) is believed to be the seat of self-respect and self-esteem. This is the point of origin for your survival intuition that guides, protects, and alerts you whenever you are in any danger, whether physically, mentally, or even emotionally. This is one of the reasons why you start to feel a little uneasy whenever you meet someone who radiates negative energy. Your eyes cannot see this energy field, but your body can immediately detect it. If you don't listen to your gut instinct or if you keep disregarding that, you are essentially violating this rather sacred energy that is present within you.

Are you wondering how your intuition is related to your self-esteem your self-respect? Well, you only listen to your gut when you start respecting and believing in yourself. If you don't have any confidence in yourself and your abilities, you tend to ignore the little voice in your head. Only when you start believing in yourself, the actions you take, and the opinions you have will you be able to strengthen your intuition. To develop your empathic abilities, you must learn to control and regulate your emotions along with your energies.

Apart from this, you must begin to learn to trust and respect yourself.

Psychic abilities

Empaths are not just naturally intuitive, but they also have certain psychic abilities. Did you ever get a weird feeling or message about someone who is hundreds of miles away? Yes, I am talking about visions. If you have experienced any such instances, then you aren't alone! And no, you are certainly not losing your mind. All empaths are psychically attuned, and the psychic visions are quite similar to intuition. The difference between a psychic vision and intuition is that even if the person you're getting a vision about could be hundreds of miles away from you, and you still get the feeling of a peculiar sense of something the person is going through.

Perhaps the best way to explain an empath's psychic abilities is to give you an example. This happened to me a couple of months ago. One fine morning, I was going through my morning meditation routine, and I suddenly got a signal about one of my childhood friends. I was not in regular contact with this friend, and I simply ignored this signal. However, as I was going through my usual routine, I kept seeing my friend's face pop up in my mind every now and then. It wasn't just her face, but I kept getting an uneasy feeling in my gut too. So, I thought it would be a good idea to just check up on her. As it turns out, she was going through a tough time, and in fact, she was going through a nasty divorce settlement. Well, my empathic abilities stepped in at the right time, and they allowed me to help someone in need.

I'm sure after reading this; you feel better about your psychic abilities. You are just experiencing the brilliance of all the powers associated with being an empath. Don't allow others to diminish the value of these gifts or even write them off as being hogwash. You know what you experience, have some faith in yourself.

Presence

As an empath, if you spend sufficient time and get in touch with your spiritual self, you will realize that there exists a form of energy or life within you. This energy animates your body or your physical form of existence. Empaths not only know this, but they also understand that the same energy is present in others around them. This energy is found in everything in the universe. Since energy can neither be created nor destroyed, it merely changes the form it exists in. Once you accept this truth, it becomes quite easy to be with others. It is almost as if we are all sharing an invisible bond that unifies us.

As an empath, you are obviously sensitive to the energy of those around you. Most empaths usually try to shield their energy away from that of others around them. By doing this, you can start resolving your energy fields has and will show protects your personal energy field from getting overwhelmed by external energies. Maintaining distance is good, but completely shielding yourself away is not a good idea, and it seldom works. Instead of worrying about setting up a protective wall around yourself, come up with ways in which you can improve confidence in your abilities. This, in turn, makes you better equipped while communicating your needs are feelings to others.

The energy field of an empath tends to vibrate at a higher level than that of other humans. This is probably one of the reasons why empaths are capable of seeing, feeling, and understanding what others feel. Therefore, it is not surprising that being in the presence of an empath, positive energy can be healing for others.

Usually, empaths favor calm, loving, and peaceful environments. The lack of harmony and the presence of chaos or discord can make empaths rather uneasy. In fact, empaths will pretty much do everything they can to ensure that there exists some peace and harmony. They constantly try to come up with solutions to any problems they come across. You probably understand this feeling. You not only try to solve your own problems but also might try to help anyone else you come across.

Empaths are quite sensitive to all negative emotions in their environment. Violence, tragedy, or chaos has a serious effect on empaths. Even if the violent or tragic event is a part of a movie you are watching, it will have a rather profound effect on you. You cannot stand it when someone is suffering. Any pain you see somehow draws out your energy and makes you sad too. So, you have a natural tendency to help others solve their problems. When surrounded by positive energy, empaths thrive and flourish.

Heal others

By now, you might have experienced a couple of instances in your life wherein you felt like you could heal others around you. Maybe not just others, but even yourself. However, have you accepted this inherent gift of yours? A lot of people tend to shy away from their empathic abilities. This behavior often stems from the fear of being different or the fear of being ostracized by society. Well, empaths are different and have healing abilities. Learning to use these healing abilities will allow you to feel more in control of your life.

For years I tried to pretend like I didn't have any empathic abilities, or that I was completely normal. I'm not suggesting that there is anything abnormal about being an empath; it merely means you're unique. I even took pride in the fact that I was not sensitive. This made me feel completely out of tune with my emotions and feelings. This, in turn, harmed every aspect of my life. I couldn't sleep at night, I slowly started to lose focus on the work I used to do, and I felt emotionally discontented. Ignoring my empathic abilities or trying to look the other way hurt my professional as well as personal lives. If you, like me, have tried doing this, then you must have experienced some or all of these things. Once all these things happen, I realized it was time for me to accept my empathic abilities. Being an empath is a part of who you are, and you cannot ignore this part. Instead of trying to run away from this part of yourself, or pretend like it doesn't exist, embrace it with open arms. By doing this, you will not only be able to help yourself but also those around you.

Once I fully accepted my empathic abilities, I could finally see what the problem was. The problem was my self-sabotaging behavior. I took complete responsibility for all my feelings, didn't try to shield my empathic abilities, started believing in my intuition, and I started taking care of myself. By doing all these things, I could see an improvement in my overall health. It felt like a huge burden off my shoulders. My empathic abilities made me feel alive and vibrant with energy. Now that I am fully healed, I can help others. It certainly takes effort to get over all this, but you certainly can. Once you have the confidence and clarity, you'll feel more determined than you ever did in life. And trust me, this feels wonderful. So, use your ability not just to hear yourself, but those around you as well.

Creativity

Empaths are usually quite creative. You might be working in a profession that allows you to expand your creative energy. You might be a healer, an entrepreneur, or must be working in a creative field like teaching, filmmaking, or anything related to arts. Your natural ability to turn any idea into solid reality is a trait that is common to all empaths. However, this can only happen if you truly accept your empathic skills. Empaths are dreamers with the power of turning their dreams into reality. All empaths can see the world quite vividly and differently than others. One of the best ways to express this ability is through creative activities. The urge to constantly create and build is present in all empaths. So, any artistic media that gives you a chance to express your creativity will work quite well for you. By engaging your creative side, you will get a better understanding of your empathic abilities too.

Most empaths find it difficult to come to terms with their natural skills. Therefore, it isn't surprising that we tend to struggle with anxiety, depression, and fatigue from time to time. Don't shy away from your natural talents. Learn to let go of your daily troubles, protect your energy, and nourish yourself. By doing all this, you are essentially nourishing your empathic abilities and your soul in this process.

If you are an empath, then you probably have some or all of the different abilities discussed in this section. Stop trying to be like everyone else. Instead, embrace your uniqueness and start appreciating yourself for who you really are. Don't allow anyone else to tell you any different. Not everyone is blessed with the abilities you possess. Think of them as superpowers, which will help turn things around. Don't shy away from them and learn to accept yourself. Once you do this, you will become unstoppable. As your fellow empath, I understand it isn't always easy to come to terms with your skills. However, the only way to thrive and live your life to the fullest is to accept yourself.

Types of Empaths

The ability to place yourself in other's shoes is known as empathy. Empaths can feel whatever emotion or feelings others feel as if it is their own. For instance, if your colleague at work is heartbroken that his beloved pet died, then your empathy allows you to feel his grief. You do not just experience the emotion, but it might also feel like it's your own emotion. This heightens the sense of positive or negative emotion you feel.

There are some empaths who can easily pick up on the emotions of others; then there are those who can identify the issue that's troubling others. Likewise, some empaths have a strong bond with nature, and some are blessed with a rather strong sense of intuition. All these abilities are common to empaths. However, every individual is unique, and therefore, the extent of their abilities also varies. There are various types of empaths, and each of these empaths has certain specific abilities. Simply put, different skills are magnified in different empaths according to the type of empathy they possess.

In this section, you'll learn about the different types of empaths and their abilities.

Emotional empaths

Of all the different types of empaths are ever come across; emotional empaths are the most common ones. As the name suggests, emotional empaths can quickly pick up on the emotions of those around them. If you are an emotional empath, you cannot only identify other's emotions, but you start experiencing them as if they were your own. As an emotional empath, don't be surprised if you deeply experienced the feeling of others in your own emotional body. Did you ever experience a profound emotion that seemed to spring on you out of nowhere? Or did you have any experiences where you knew the emotion you were experiencing what not your own? If yes, then it is quite likely that you are an emotional empath.

Both positive, as well as negative emotions, tend to have a profound effect on emotional empaths. For instance, by being around those who radiate joy, it will lift your spirits and heighten your energy vibrancy. As mentioned in the earlier example at the beginning of this section, an emotional empath can become extremely sad when around someone who is experiencing grief. So, if your colleague is grieving over his pet's death, you will experience his grief, as if it's your own grief.

You must start differentiating between the emotions you pick from others and your own emotions. This practice is quintessential for emotional empaths, for the sake of their wellbeing. If you are tired of feeling like you aren't in control or feeling drained out all the time, then setting up certain emotional boundaries is essential. You don't have to turn off your empathic abilities; you must merely learn to identify your emotions and distinguish them from those of others.

Physical empaths

Physical empaths are also known as medical empaths. Physical empaths can easily pick up on the energy from other people's bodies. They seem to possess an intuitive ability, which allows them to understand what ails the other person. Individuals with this type of empathy are natural healers. Opting for a profession either in conventional or alternative medicine is a good idea for physical or medical empaths. They might be able to see any blockages in energy or feel the presence of any ailment in the physical bodies of those around them.

The way emotional empaths tend to feel others' emotions as their own, physical empaths might be able to experience others' physical symptoms in their own bodies. This can be rather detrimental to your own health. However, it can help reduce the severity of symptoms in those you treat. All those who suffer from chronic illnesses such as autoimmune disorders, chronic arthritis, or fibromyalgia might find it helpful when around physical empaths. However, you must learn how to manage this ability of yours and taking some training in a specific type of healing can come in handy. Also, if you train yourself to become a healer, you can hone this gift you possess.

Geomantic empaths

These empaths are also known as environmental or place empaths. If you possess this type of empathy, then you have a natural affinity to the environment. If certain places make you experience extreme emotions, positive and negative ones, for a reason you cannot discern, then you are probably a geomantic empath. You might find yourself drawn to specific places of sacred power like stones, places of worship, or even groves. Apart from this, you might be quite sensitive to the history of the place too. So, any happy, sad, or devastating occurrences in a specific spot will come to you as feelings. Your inherent attunement to the natural world means that you will be saddened whenever landscapes are destroyed or if a spot is being damaged. Any damage to a physical location will make you experience negative emotions.

The best way to charge your energy is by spending time outdoors in nature. Ensure that you fill up your living accommodations with plenty of plants and other natural materials. As long as there is harmony in your surroundings, you will thrive.

Plant empaths

As the name suggests, these empaths are finely attuned to plants or flora. It also seems like plant empaths have an inherent understanding of the needs of plants. Plant empaths are those who are blessed with a green thumb! If you like spending time in nature, like gardening, or spend time involved in activities related to plants, you will thrive. In fact, a lot of plant empaths use this gift of theirs to work in gardens, landscapes, parks, or anywhere else they can use this gift. They tend to receive direct guidance from the plants they nurture and care for. To recharge yourself, spend time in contact with trees and plants. The simple act of meditating in a garden or under a tree is a good idea. Also, start placing plants in your living accommodations to feel better.

Animal empaths

As the name suggests, these empaths are finely attuned to the needs of animals. They share a natural and strong bond with animals. I will not be surprised if animal empaths prefer spending time with animals than in the company of humans. In fact, most of these empaths tend to devote their energy toward taking care of animals. They intuitively know what animals need and might even be able to understand what animals require telepathically. So, spending time with animals will help recharge your energy field and make you feel better. If you want to refine your gift, then pursuing a career related to taking care of animals might help. You can become an animal healer to put your gift to good use.

Intuitive empaths

This brings me to the final category of empaths, and they are the claircognizant empaths. These empaths are also known as intuitive empaths. As their name suggests, they are quite adept at picking up information from others by merely being around them. If you possess this kind of empathic abilities, then you will be able to gain insight into a person by glancing at them. This also means that no one can hide their true intentions from you. People tend to lie, put on an act, or a façade for the world. A claircognizant empath can see through this façade. You possess the ability to read other people's energy fields and the energy of their body projects. This kind of empaths is believed to be quite similar to telepathic empaths.

If you are an intuitive empath, then always stay in the company of those with whom you feel in sync. If your energy levels are in harmony with those around you, your empathic abilities will shine brighter. Don't allow others to trespass into your energy field.

As an empath, I know that it isn't easy to live with this gift. There will be times when you feel utterly drained out, confused, and even disoriented. By understanding the type of empathic abilities you possess, it becomes easier to manage your gift and help others.

Chapter 4: The Neuroscience Behind Empathy

Neuronal Explanations of Enhanced Empathy

I've always been fascinated by the way empathy works. Not just because I am an empath, but also my interest in psychology prompted me to learn more about the science behind empathy an empath. An empath is placed quite high on the empathic spectrum, and they're capable of feeling what is happening in other people in their own bodies. Because of this, empaths tend to feel a lot of compassion for those. However, they also get tired of all these excessive feelings the experience unless they've learned to set certain boundaries to protect their sacred energy. In this section, you will learn about the different scientific explanations about enhanced empathy. Once you understand this, it becomes easier to understand how your empathy works and the way it influences your life.

Mirror neuron system

When you think about empathy, the first explanation that might come to your mind is that your heart goes out whenever you see someone in pain. Wait, you must be thinking that empathy comes from your heart. Well, empathy stems from your brain, just like the happiness you experience. There are certain neurons that are responsible for triggering feelings of compassion. These cells are the reason why people can mirror emotions. Apart from this, the specialized cells are also responsible for your ability to feel someone else's pain, joy, or even fears. As an empath, your network of mirror neurons is hyper-responsive. This is the reason why you are capable of resonating with other's feelings and emotions on a deeper level than an average human being.

You must be wondering how all of this cause. Well, external events usually trigger the pathway of mirror neurons in your brain. For instance, when your partner experiences sadness, you experience it too. If your child is crying, you will feel sad too. When your colleague is extremely happy, you tend to feel happy. Psychopaths, narcissists, and sociopaths are on the other end of the spectrum. When I say the other end of the spectrum, I mean that they suffer from a severe deficiency of empathy. It essentially means that they lack the ability to feel any empathy the way normal people do. This is caused because of an underactive mirror neuron network in their brain. If you ever cross paths with anyone who has an empty deficiency, you must be quite careful. These people are energy vampires, and they are incapable of loving anyone unconditionally.

Electromagnetic fields

Did you know that your brain, along with your heart, tends to give out electromagnetic fields? Does this sound like something right out of a science fiction movie? Well, it is not science fiction, and it is simple biology. These electromagnetic fields present around you tend to provide information about your thoughts and emotions. Every human being has a personal electromagnetic field. After all, we are all made up of energy, and energy keeps vibrating at different frequencies. Empaths are usually extremely sensitive to this information, and they can become rather overwhelmed because of all this energy around them. Likewise, empaths also have a stronger emotional, as well as a physical, response to any changes in the Sun and the Earth. As a highly sensitive empath, you must become aware of the simple fact that simple planetary movements of the earth and the sun tend to affect your personal electromagnetic field.

Emotional contagion

Another interesting finding that I came across, which helped improve my understanding of empaths, is a concept known as emotional contagion. A lot of people are capable of picking up on emotions and feelings of all those people around them. Did you ever see a group of children playing together? If one of them starts laughing uncontrollably, within the next couple of moments, all the children will be laughing. Likewise, when one infant cries in a hospital ward, all the other infants in the ward also start crying. If one of your colleagues starts expressing his anxiety about losing his job, this anxiety will quickly spread in all the employees. The phenomenon of emotional contagion is prevalent in all situations. For instance, one of the most common examples of this would be the way the stock market functions.

When used investors start selling their stocks, all the other investors in the market follow suit. When in groups, people easy catch feelings from others in the group. This ability to sync your feelings with those around you is quintessential for establishing good relationships and life. Are you wondering what this has got to do with empathy? Well, keep this in mind whenever you are interacting with others. By being mindful of all those you interact with, you can ensure that your circle consists of positive people who uplift you instead of the negative or toxic ones who bring you down. My advice is that if you know one of your loved ones is going through a rather challenging face in life, then you must work on granting yourself. As an empath, your emotions are easily altered by those around you. If you are careful, you'll quickly lose control of your thoughts and emotions. Not just that, all the emotions of those around you will drain you out.

Increased dopamine sensitivity

Do you know what dopamine is? Dopamine is a common neurotransmitter that increases the activity of the neurons present in your brain that are associated with triggering feelings of pleasure. When compared to an extravert empath, introverted empaths usually have a higher level of sensitivity towards dopamine. It essentially means that introverted empaths don't need much of dopamine to feel happy. A little dopamine can make them feel quite joyful. This is of likely reason why I think they're quite happy spending time by themselves. By meditating, relaxing, reading, or indulging in any activity that they enjoy, they feel quite good about themselves. They don't need to be present in social settings to derive happiness. This is in complete contrast with extravert empaths. Extrovert empaths thrive when there are in huge crowds. In fact, they tend to get a dopamine rush when they're in social gatherings.

The more, the merrier, seems to be their mantra in life. By understanding whether you are an introvert or an extravert empath, you can work on energizing and protecting your empathic energies.

Synaesthesia

The final finding I came across is probably the most compelling of the lot. This is a concept known as mirror-touch synesthesia. When two different senses are paired together in your brain, it results in a neurological condition known as synesthesia. For instance, you might experience a specific taste or smell whenever you read. Or perhaps you see vibrant colors whenever you listen to music. As absurd as this sounds, this is quite real. Did you know that Isaac Newton and Billy Joel were synesthetes? The people who have this condition are capable of feeling various emotions and sensations of other people in their own bodies as if they were their own emotional sensations.

This is perhaps the most convincing neurological explanation that is about the way an empath feels.

Studies about Empathy

After going through the information provided in the previous section, it is safe to assume that empathy depends on one's mental makeup. It might seem like some people are inherently more empathetic than others. Is this true? Can some people be more compassionate than others? What are the different habits or life experiences that trigger and reinforce undesirable traits on the other end of the spectrum like narcissism or selfishness?

Research related to the neural network and empathy is still ongoing. However, from amongst all the different studies conducted up until now, I think there are two that stand out. The first study was conducted by the Max Planck Institute for Human and Cognitive Brain Sciences, and the second study was conducted by the University of Chicago. Both these studies offer an explanation along with scientific proof and reasoning to show the neurobiological roots of empathy.

The neuroscience of empathy

On October 9, 2013, a study was published in the Journal of Neuroscience by the researchers of the Max Planck Institute for Human and Cognitive Brain Sciences. The aim of this research was to try to identify that the tendency of being egocentric does come naturally to humans. But a specific region of the brain recognizes the absence of empathy and fixes it. This region of the human brain is known as the supramarginal gyrus. If the supramarginal gyrus doesn't optimally function or whenever humans have to make extremely quick decisions, the researchers discovered that one's ability to be empathic reduces drastically. This region of the brain allows us to differentiate between our current emotional state and that of those around us. The supramarginal gyrus is also responsible for triggering feelings of compassion and empathy.

The cerebral cortex includes the supramarginal gyrus. It is situated at the point of intersection between the temporal, parietal, and frontal lobes. Tania Singer was heading this research team. Their research was based on the premise that humans tend to use themselves as a yardstick and tend to project themselves on others while assessing the emotional state of their fellow humans. Cognition research already makes all this abundantly clear. However, little is known about its applicability on an emotional level. Until this research, it was a widely accepted belief that one's own emotional state can easily distort our perception of others' emotions, especially if the said emotions are different from one's own emotions. However, no attempts were made to measure this kind of emotional egocentricity.

Our ability to distinguish our perception of others from our own self-perception is because of the right supramarginal gyrus. During the course of the research, a disruption was caused in the neurons present in this part of the brain. This disruption affected the participants, and they found it rather difficult to stop themselves from projecting their own feelings and perspectives onto others. The accuracy of decisions made by the participants also reduced when they had to decide quickly.

It becomes harder to empathize with someone else's suffering whenever you are nestled in the lap of luxury. One's ability to empathize with others' suffering reduces whenever you are in a comfortable or an agreeable situation. When your supramarginal gyrus isn't functioning like properly, then your ability to place yourself in other's shoes decreases. To test this neurobiological reaction, a perception experiment was used by the Max Planck researchers. For the sake of the research, participants were exposed to unpleasant or pleasant visual as well as tactile stimuli simultaneously.

For instance, a little slime was placed on the participant 1's hand, and this participant was shown a picture of maggots. Participant number 2 could feel soft fur or fleece under her hand hands and was then shown a picture of a puppy. For the sake of this experiment, the tactile stimuli had to be combined. If these stimuli weren't combined, then the participants would have responded to the situation using their rational brains while their feelings were excluded from the equation. The participants, who were working in groups of two, could also see the different stimuli their partners were exposed to as well.

After this, the two participants were asked to analyze their own emotions when compared to those of their test partners. The participants found it rather easy to assess their partner's emotions when they were also exposed to the same kind of negative or positive stimuli.

The participant who had to deal with a disagreeable or unpleasant situation could easily understand how unpleasant her partner would have felt at sight and the feel of maggots and slime. Differences in opinions cropped up when one of the partners was subjected to pleasant stimuli while the other had to deal with unpleasant stimuli. In this situation, the capacity of the partners to feel empathy decreased. The participants who were subjected to pleasant experiences assessed their partner's negative experiences as being less severe than it actually was. The opposite of this was true too. The participants who had unpleasant experiences rated their partner's positive experiences less positively.

Until this study was conducted, different models of social neuroscience were based on the assumption that humans used their own emotions as a reference for displaying empathy. However, this would only work when you are either in the same or a neutral state as the other person. Otherwise, your brain uses its supramarginal gyrus for counteracting and correcting the tendencies humans have for self-centered perceptions of the pain, discomfort, or suffering experienced by others.

Lack of empathy- neurological basis

What is the first thing that pops into your head when you hear the term psychopath? You probably think about serial killers like Ted Bundy or even the Son of Sam. Do you know what psychopathy really means? It is a clinically classified personality disorder wherein the individual is incapable of feeling any remorse or empathy whatsoever. Apart from this, psychopaths are often shallow, manipulative, glib, and callous. From the previous study, it is quite clear that empathy is triggered by a neurological process in the brain. When it comes to a psychopath, there is no change in those areas of their brain responsible for showing empathy whenever they see others in pain or discomfort. Also, all the different areas of the brain that collectively help process information and make compassionate decisions stay inactive.

A study was published in the Frontiers in Human Neuroscience, 2013 by the Department of Psychology at the University of Chicago related to the neurobiological roots related to psychopathic behavior. Whenever an individual imagines any pain being inflicted on themselves, different areas of the brain become active. These areas include; the anterior midcingulate cortex, the right amygdala, the anterior insula, and the somatosensory cortex. When the psychopathic participants of the study imagined the pain to themselves, the neural response in their brain was quite normal. However, there was an unusual increase in their neural activity in these regions. This led the researchers to conclude that psychopathic individuals are quite sensitive to the thought of pain, but they cannot place themselves in other's shoes or feel their pain.

These regions failed to show any activity when the participants were asked to imagine others in pain. Here comes the sadistic twist, when they thought of others in pain, there was increased neural activity in the ventral striatum region of their brains. This is the region responsible for regulating pleasure felt by an individual. PCL-R, a popular tool used for assessing the degree of psychopathic tendencies, was used to test the participants. Based on the results of this assessment, all the participants were grouped into different categories of psychopathic tendencies- weak, moderate, and high. Approximately 40 participants were included in each of these categories.

The rate of psychopathy in prisons was significantly higher than the prevalent rate in the average population, according to previous research. The rate of psychopathy in the average population is about 1%, whereas it was as high as 23% in prisons. To get a better understanding of the neurological reasons for this empathy dysfunction in psychopaths, neuroscientist performed MRI scans on 121 inmates housed in a medium-security facility.

The participants of this study were shown different visual scenarios depicting physical pain. These visual depictions ranged from a finger stuck in a door to a toe that's stuck under a heavy object. Then the participants were asked to visualize that these accidents happened to themselves or others. They were also shown certain control images like a hand placed on a doorknob and other images that didn't show any painful situations.

The researchers of this study believed that by understanding the neurobiological roots of empathy and psychopathy, they could come up with intervention programs that can help individuals with psychopathic tendencies. By concentrating on neural networks, different therapeutic tools can be created to improve empathy in humans, especially in those displaying psychopathic behavior and indulging in mildly violent crimes. The authors of this study came to the conclusion that cognitive-behavioral therapies can be used on some psychopaths and open up doors for their reformation.

Conclusion

You must be wondering what conclusion you were supposed to arrive at from these studies. Well, the conclusion is that there are different things you can do to make your brain more empathetic.

Neuroscience provides helpful insight into the way the human mind works and helps us understand it better. Armed with this knowledge, it becomes easier to make such decisions or choices that help reshape one's neural circuits and alter the way you interact with others. Neuroplasticity can help rewire your brain's neural circuitry which can make you more empathetic and compassionate. If you want to improve these tendencies, then you must make some conscious and consistent effort. You must strive to put yourself in other's shoes to reinforce the way your neural networks process emotions and situations. Only when you understand how others feel will you be able to show genuine empathy. There is no simple or easy answer to how you can elevate your empathetic responses. I think it is all about making conscious choices daily while help promotes empathy.

There are different techniques you can use, like mindfulness meditation like LKM (loving-kindness meditation), altruism, by volunteering, engaging in physical activities, and by displaying pro-social behaviors. The common aspect of all these activities is that you must become more mindful and conscious of the way you think and present yourself. If you feel like you need to work on improving your empathy, then you must try these exercises. Don't expect any miraculous results overnight, and it takes a lot of conscious effort, consistency, and patience. It isn't something you can do once or twice a week and expect the problem to be resolved. It is about developing healthy habits.

When you practice LKM, it helps rewire your brain and promote all those neural connections that are associated with empathy. You are literally rewiring your brain to become more empathic. You will learn about the LKM exercise in the subsequent sections. Physical activity is not just good for your body, but it helps calm your mind too. Whenever you exercise, your body releases endorphins and other feel-good hormones while restricting the production of stress-inducing hormones like cortisol. When your body is pumped with these happy hormones, you will start feeling better. It also helps you become more aware of the connection between your body and mind.

Including any form of daily physical activity can help improve your empathic abilities. For instance, when you are engaged in high-intensity interval training, you are required to push through all the physical discomfort you feel and keep going. The suffering you endure not only strengthens your body, but it helps you feel more empathetic about human suffering. Only when you experience pain will you be able to show empathy towards others in pain.

When you make it a daily habit of consciously engaging and experiencing something that isn't naturally agreeable to you, your body and mind become tough. This makes you more sensitive to what pain means. By letting go of your sedentary and comfort-filled life, and going on a run, you get a chance to connect to the essence of human struggle that's widely prevalent in this world.

Volunteering is one of the simplest ways in which you can become more empathetic toward others.

Whenever you volunteer and help those who are less fortunate than you, you get a chance to gain some personal experience. Working in close quarters with such people can make you feel grateful for all that you have. Apart from this, it also reinforces the feelings of empathy in your brain. By actively helping others to reduce their suffering, you will start to feel better about yourself.

Exercises

Practicing LKM (loving-kindness meditation) daily is quite helpful. I suggest that you spend at least ten minutes to practice this simple exercise. You don't need any props for this exercise.

- Find a calm, relaxing, and quiet spot for yourself. Get rid of all distractions and keep all gadgets away. Make yourself comfortable; you can either lie down on the ground or even sit in a chair.

- Now, it is time to gather all your thoughts and concentrate on your breathing. As you start inhaling, imagine that positivity is rushing into your body, and when you exhale, visualize that all negative thoughts are leaving your mind.

- Now, it is time to redirect some loving and compassionate thoughts toward others. Start by showing a little compassion to yourself.

- Appreciate yourself and send some positive energy and thoughts your way.

- After this, it is time to send loving and compassionate thoughts to your family members, friends, and other loved ones. The power of positive thinking and energy must never be overlooked.

- If you feel like you are having any troubles with someone or have some unresolved conflicts, then send some loving and kind thoughts toward that person too. You never know what others are going through, and everyone can use a little help every now and then.

- Start sending happy thoughts and positive energy towards all those who are suffering. It helps reduce the negativity present in the world.

- Now, it is time to forgive yourself for any mistakes you made and forget about it. Let go of any unkind thoughts you have about yourself — practice self-love and self-compassion.

- End the meditation, slowly open your eyes, and get back to your daily life.

Chapter 5: Dealing With Friends And Family

Raised By Narcissistic Parents

Children look up to their parents for guidance, support, confidence, and love. Being raised by narcissistic parents means that a child is denied all these things. This not only makes for an unpleasant childhood, but it also means such children tend to develop various beliefs and coping mechanisms that help them survive childhood. However, these coping mechanisms, along with misplaced beliefs, are often carried on into adulthood by them. As an empath, I can only imagine how traumatic it would've been not to get everything that all the other kids your age for caring for the parents. I am not talking about any expensive commodities or toys, talking about the nurturing support and love of parents.

Being raised by narcissistic parents is never pleasant. According to shamanism, this kind of upbringing leads to soul loss. Shamanism is native to various native cultures across the globe. Soul loss is described as an individual's inability to stay in touch with one's soul and form bonds with others because of the buildup of unresolved traumas or fears. Soul loss sounds quite tragic, doesn't it? If you want to heal yourself, then it is important to explore every issue you faced growing up. While doing this, don't with demise yourself and, instead, learn to identify the cause of any pain you experience today. There will always be a blockage in your energy if you don't address these issues from your past.

Codependency

Narcissists thrive on codependency. If you had a narcissistic parent or parents, then I'm pretty certain that you probably heard sentences like, "don't leave me," "I cannot survive without you," or "I need you." A child must depend on his parents, but it must not be the other way around, at least not during the initial stages of childhood. This might have made it quite impossible for you to gain any independence in your life. After all, most of your time and attention will be dedicated to making your parents' life easier. As an empath, it is quite likely that you spent all your attention and effort to cater to your parents' needs instead of tending to yourself.

Guilt

Guilt is a rather powerful emotion, and in the hands of a narcissist, it can be easily weaponized. Narcissists often use controlling techniques to get what they want. If you tend to agree to something your parents had or tried to ascertain your independence, you might have been a guilt trip for doing this. You might have been told things like, "I have sacrificed so much for you," or "I have done so much for you; how can you do this to me?" Said empaths easily feel guilty about things, a narcissistic parent would have used your guilt to gain your complete obedience. You were essentially putty in your parent's hands.

Conditional loving

True love must always be unconditional. Parents are supposed to love their children unconditionally, and if this love comes with many conditions, it causes a severe imbalance of power in the relationship. There might have been instances in your childhood where your parents withdrew love quite easily. You probably got attention and love only when you did things to please them. If you did anything that they didn't want or failed to do what they want, they might have withheld their love. This might have given you the impression that you would be loved only if you listened to others and fulfilled their wishes. Love isn't supposed to be conditional, and if it is, it's often a sign of a toxic relationship.

Getting even

Punishment might have been quite common to grow up. When you read something that your parents didn't want or did something wrong according to them, you might have on their punishment. Even the slightest misstep would have cost you dearly. Narcissists have a rather petty way of dealing with things. They believe in the concept of caring even. For instance, your parents might have deliberately hidden your favorite toy because you forgot to take out the garbage in the morning.

No boundaries

Narcissists don't understand the concept of personal boundaries. Even if they managed to understand this concept, they could not respect the idea of personal space. As an empath, having personal boundaries is quintessential for your wellbeing. When these boundaries are violated, empaths experience internal chaos. If the concept of private space sounds foreign to you, it probably because of growing up with narcissistic parents, you never had any private space. Here narcissistic father or mother could probably go through your private belongings or even your room without giving it a second thought.

Unhealthy competition

Narcissists love being the center of attention, and whenever this attention is taken away from them, they cannot stand it. They not only like being the center of attention, but they want constant attention. This usually creates unhealthy competition. There is no space for unhealthy competition in a parent-child relationship. A narcissistic parent would constantly try to one-up their children. If you did something nice, it is quite likely that your narcissistic parent tried to do something even better. I wouldn't be surprised if this created some unhealthy ideas about competition in your head.

Own your accomplishments

As already mentioned, narcissists love attention. Even if someone complimented you about your achievements, it's quite likely that your parents would swoop in and take the credit for your accomplishments. By doing this, they essentially tried shifting the attention from you to themselves. For instance, if someone congratulated you about winning the spell the completion at school, it's quite likely that your parents used to butt in and say, "oh well, she gets it from me! I was always academically-oriented."

Constant lying

One of the simplest ways to manipulate someone is through lying, and a narcissist understands this thoroughly. A narcissistic parent would try to control their children or take advantage of them in some way or the other by lying to them. This constant lying you were subjected to can make you feel rather suspicious of all the people you interact with in your life.

Poor listeners

If it weren't about them, a narcissist would not want to listen to anything. Even if your narcissistic parents listen to you about your feelings, they perhaps don't care about them. Such behavior might have made you believe that you must never share your feelings with anyone. Not just this, but it might have also made you feel like your emotions and options didn't matter. The denial of validation can dent anyone's self-confidence. Even if by chance you narcissistic parents managed to listen to you, they probably made fun of the things you say or might have shifted the focus onto themselves again. Somehow, regardless of the issues you faced as a child, it became a pity party for your narcissistic parent.

Explicit control

Covert narcissism and passive-aggressive behaviors can be quite manipulative. However, narcissistic parents also exert explicit control over their children. You might have heard sentences like, "you'll be punished if you don't listen to me." The threat of being punished might have compelled you to listen to whatever your narcissistic parents wanted from you.

Constant insults

Dealing with constant insults might have been a normal occurrence in your childhood. You were probably berated constantly, harassed, or even humiliated on a regular basis. Your narcissistic parents might have figured out some of your insecurities and use them against you. A narcissist doesn't hesitate to throw a low punch, and hitting below the belt is quite normal for them.

You were the parent

No child is supposed to be the parent. After all, what are parents for if the child is supposed to do the parenting? As a child with narcissistic parents, it is pretty certain that you were expected to parent your parent. You might have been required to step into the role of a surrogate parent and take care of their needs instead of it being the other way around. Your entire childhood probably revolved around your narcissistic parent.

Gaslighting

A common tactic of psychological manipulation favored by a narcissist is gaslighting. What it essentially means is that the narcissist tries to make you feel like you are losing your sanity to gain control over you. This means you start questioning yourself even when you know you are right. By making you feel like you're going crazy, the narcissist is deliberately gaining the upper hand in the relationship. If your childhood was riddled with self-doubt, it is quite likely that you carried this self-doubt into your adulthood as well.

Golden child

Narcissistic parents tend to have a favorite child. I know parents aren't supposed to favor just one of their kids, but this is sadly true when it comes to narcissists. This might have happened to you if you have any siblings. Your narcissistic parents might have had a favorite or a golden child, and the family scapegoat. Simply put, the narcissistic parents tend to think of one child is being perfect, and the other one as the family black sheep. If you were the family black sheep, then whatever went wrong was probably blamed on you. This blame was fixed regardless of whether it was your personal doing or not. These roles are not necessarily fixed, and they might have kept changing from one sibling to the other. After all, it doesn't matter as long as the narcissists get their way.

Intense reactions

A narcissist usually suffers from a sense of heightened self-importance. Narcissists truly believe that they can never be wrong, and they are always right. So, even the slightest criticism from you might have on there. Did you ever criticize any of your parents? If yes, then what was the usual reaction? If either of your parents were a narcissist, then it is quite likely that they reacted in an extreme manner. It could and wrapped in a screaming match, or they might have even tried to punish you physically.

Lack of empathy

In the same way, the sun is believed to be the center of the universe; the narcissist believes he is the center of the universe. According to narcissists, they're the only ones who are capable of feeling and experiencing emotions. In fact, they are often surprised that others can also think and feel for themselves. Therefore, having any conversations about your feelings might have been quite rare in a narcissistic household. All that you narcissistic parents seem to be interested in was on feelings and not yours. So, the concept of empathy was never taught to you.

Projection

For instance, if you were having an argument, your narcissistic parent might have hysterically screamed at you, "how dare you to talk like this to me? Go to your room immediately. We will talk once you stop screaming at me." Even if you weren't screaming, the entire blame shifted onto you. Narcissistic parents have a terrible habit of projecting their bad behavior on to the children. Even if they are the ones at fault, they will turn things around and blame the kids for the same.

Perfect family

Narcissists believe in superficial appearances. So, maintaining the facade of being the perfect family might have been quite important to your narcissistic parent. In fact, I'm pretty sure they would have gone to great lengths to make sure that others thought of you as allowing family. You might have been aware of this little game they liked to play, but might have held your tongue not to incur their wrath.

Growing up with narcissistic parents might have been a nightmare. If you're still living with them, you are still stuck in the same nightmare. As an empath, dealing with a narcissist might make you feel like you're lost all hope in life. However, the good news is, you can take control of your life right now. If you feel like you're stuck in a toxic relationship, it is time to sever all ties and wrong. You must make yourself a priority and stop worrying about others for a change. Also, any issues that you experience as an empath today is probably because of the unreasonable conditioning he was subjected to growing up. A parent-child relationship is one of the most sacred bonds there is and is the parent who violates this bond. Obviously, it creates dents in a child's self-image.

Any trust issues that you have, self-doubt, inability to open up to others, or maybe wrong assumptions about love are all due to the manipulative treatment doled out to you by your narcissistic parents. If you identify with any or all of the different aspects of the relationship discussed in this section, then you are a victim of narcissistic abuse. If you want to heal yourself, you must accept this fact, make peace with it, and take steps to prevent the same from happening in the future.

Signs of Narcissistic with Parents

Appearance

Narcissists are quite superficial. One of the top priorities for any narcissist is to maintain appearances. Your narcissistic parents might not have cared much about all that you had to say, but they certainly cared a lot about how you look. Not just your physical appearance, but also the impression that others had about you. They love the idea of perfection, and when others perceive them as being perfect, they feel quite elated. In fact, narcissists would go to great lengths to do all this. Maintaining the façade of a perfect or an ideal family would have been extremely important to your parents. Regardless of how unhealthy or toxic the relationship was, they never would have wanted others to know about all this.

Children have no voice

If life were a fashion show, then the narcissist would be a showstopper, the model, as well as the designer. Narcissists love attention and will go to great lengths to ensure that the spotlight is never taken away from them. This means that narcissistic parents wouldn't be quite concerned with what their kids have to say. All that matters is their opinion and their needs. Narcissists also tend to believe that their opinion is the only one that matters; after all, they are always right. Therefore, a narcissistic mother would never think about asking her children what they feel of what they would want to do. Likewise, a narcissistic father might not care what his child feels.

Neglecting their kids

Since narcissists believe that they are superior to others, they also possess a heightened feeling of entitlement. They live in a bubble where they assume that everyone in this world is there to cater to their needs. They always try to fulfill their needs. By hook or by crook, they will always get what they want. It doesn't matter who gets hurt in this process as long as their needs and wishes fulfilled. Often their needs are quite selfish and don't take into consideration those feelings or emotions.

They are never wrong

Narcissists like to view themselves as being the epitome of perfection. Maybe its perfection in terms of looks, family, or even friends, they desire perfection. Since narcissists believe that they are perfect, they also assume that there never wrong. After all, how could someone be perfect if they made mistakes? As messed up as this sounds, this is how a narcissist thinks. Therefore, narcissistic parents would never accept their mistakes. They would never shoulder their responsibilities and would always expect others to do this for them. If something does go wrong, the narcissistic parent would conveniently shift all the burden onto the child's shoulders. After a while, this kind of conditioning can make children believe that they are the ones at fault. Apart from this, children might also start failing that they are the only thing that's not perfect and their parent's life.

Narcissistic Siblings

Dealing with narcissistic siblings is almost as dramatic as dealing with narcissistic parents. Dealing with any sort of narcissist in any relationship you have in life can be quite challenging. If you're surrounded by narcissists in a household, your empathic abilities will take a backseat. Growing up with a narcissistic sibling would have been quite traumatic. If you're still dealing with a narcissistic sibling, then I am sure you dread meeting them.

The extreme need for attention

Narcissists not only love attention, but you also need constant attention. They seek validation from others, and only when they get this validation, do they feel good. Even if this validation doesn't count for much, it is sufficient to fuel a narcissists' ego. As an empath, you might have been quite supportive and understanding of everything that your sibling did and said. Your narcissistic sibling, on the other hand, might have taken the sympathy of yours for granted. Empaths always try to make others feel better. So, if narcissists want attention and praise, they can always count on empaths. The need for attention that narcissists have is almost like a black hole. Regardless of all the positivity, you keep fueling it; there will always be space for more. The relationship you share with your sibling would have been quite one-sided. As an empath, it is in your nature to keep giving and giving, and as a narcissist, it is on your sibling's nature to demand more and more.

The belief of innate superiority

The world of the narcissist is quite black-and-white. Things exist at the extreme ends of the spectrum, and shades of grey don't exist. In the world of the narcissist, everything falls into two categories-good or bad, right or wrong, and superior or inferior. There is nothing in between. The only hierarchy that exists is where the narcissist is at the top of the list. This is the only place where they feel safe. The narcissist always has to be the best, always right and do everything their own way. They laughed, being in control and controlling others. Narcissists are often quite good at what they do, and this feels their inherent sense of superiority. Likewise, they can also be the absolute worst and still experience the same sense of superiority. They also feel like they're entitled to receiving soothing concern from others and will demand that you make things right even if it was not your fault. So, if you ever had a fight with this sibling, the blame would always be on you, and your sibling would always be right.

Self-delusion

The way narcissistic parents love being perfect, even your narcissistic sibling loves the same. They have an extremely high need for perfection. Narcissists believe that they must be perfect, that others around them must be perfect. Everything in their life must go as they have planned, and everyone must play the roles they have been assigned by the narcissist. This demand is not only ridiculous, but it is also excruciatingly impossible to fulfill. Therefore, narcissists often feel miserable and dissatisfied. The demand for perfection makes the narcissist complain incessantly.

Verbal abuse, belittling, ridicule, and humiliation

A narcissistic sibling would try to gain dominance over others by resorting to verbal abuse. Verbal abuse includes unnecessary humiliation and ridicule. Your narcissistic sibling might ridicule you in public or belittle you by preying on any of your known weaknesses. By doing all this, the narcissistic sibling is essentially trying to gain control over you. Since your sibling knows your vulnerabilities, be prepared that one time or the other, they will be used against you. Even things you share that you sibling in strict confidence but become public knowledge. Narcissists don't hesitate and will go to great lengths as long as it allows them to be in control.

Why Empath Can Struggle In Friendship

For highly sensitive empaths, friendships are not easy to maintain. It's not that empaths are antisocial; it merely means that they have certain unique needs in a relationship. Some empaths might find it quite difficult to connect with people. While others might be able to establish a good rapport but would fail to maintain the relationship later. I would like to give you examples of two friends of mine who were both empaths. One of my friends used to complain that she is to feel like an outsider because all the people she met then didn't have the kind of depth she desired. Another friend of mine used to comment on how she had a strong relationship with a friend. But that friend never seemed to put in as much effort as she did to nurture the relationship. All this left my friends feeling like they're stuck in a one-sided relationship.

Easily overwhelmed

Socializing means spending time in public. Social gatherings and spending time in crowded places can be quite overwhelming for an empath. All the things that others seem to enjoy might not be pleasurable for an empath, and that's fine. If you are like me, I am sure that it takes every ounce of energy you have to spend any length of time in a place that is visually stimulating and extremely noisy. So, spending hours dancing at a club might not be your cup of tea, and that's all right. You might enjoy live music and might love going out once in a while, but this might not be something you'd like to do every day of the week. If your friends are not highly sensitive like you are, then they might not understand what you are going through. A regular environment that is pleasurable to others might be overstimulating for a sensitive person.

Deep connections

A highly sensitive empath would not like to waste time engaging in small talk. In fact, engaging in the small talk will make you feel quite tired and drained of your energy. Such interactions seem rather shallow and meaningless trampled. I usually desire to form deep and authentic connections with people I come across. Instead of engaging in a menial conversation about how the weather is, I would rather spend hours talking about the wonders of life and personal growth with a kindred spirit. It might sound quite familiar to you, but it isn't always possible to form such a deep connection with everyone you come across in life. It is okay to have a small yet close circle of friends. You don't have to worry about maintaining a large social group. If deep connections matter to you, then work on strengthening your relationships with a select few and cherish them.

Societal norms

Usually, highly sensitive people don't like following any societal norms, and the same stands true for an empath as well. All empaths are capable of sensing all subtleties of energy that are present around them. This ability of theirs allows them to determine whenever someone is inauthentic around them just to fit in. An average human being might not realize it, but empaths can notice even those emotions are others are actively trying to mask or cover. Empaths start to feel rather disconnected from those around them when others refuse to take off their masks. Apart from this, empaths also detest the idea of having to pretend to be someone they are not. All this can become quite challenging, especially when you notice that you're in a friendship with someone who seems to be pretending all the time. Such relationships can easily drain you of your energy.

Lack of reciprocation

Empaths are great listeners and have a nurturing nature. They certainly are amazing skills that a person can have. However, if an empath isn't careful, it creates a relationship where the empath is always the listener. In fact, I will not be surprised if you end up forming such relationships wherein you're the only one who keeps listening all the time, and the other person doesn't even reciprocate. The lack of reciprocation will quickly work against an empath. By doing this, you are essentially absorbing all the problems of those around you. Remember, it is okay to listen, but it is not okay to become an emotional sponge. If you keep on absorbing someone else's energy all the time, your personal energy levels will be severely harmed. Apart from this, it is an empaths nature to give a person the benefit of the doubt. In fact, I think that we all do this a little too easily. Regardless of the fact that we can see when someone is not authentic, empaths are extremely patient and often take a while to understand that the friendship they are in is not leveled.

Isolation

Most empaths usually lean towards introversion. This is primarily tied to the way an empath processes emotions and feelings. Being in public spaces or spending time in crowded locations too long is always mentally and emotionally draining for an empath. Attending social obligations and spending time in an overstimulating environment is not good for the personal energy of an empath. So, they prefer spending time by themselves. If you are like me, then I fully understand the need to sneak away from all the crowds and spend some time in nature or by myself or even just restrict myself to my living room. The desire for isolation and the need for it might not be answered by everyone. People might think that you're antisocial, shy, or just not interested in meeting others. Even if this is not true, solitude is quintessential for the overall wellbeing of an empath.

Maintaining friendships can become a result of this need. For instance, your friends keep making plans, they keep inviting you, and you keep canceling for one reason or the other. If you keep at it long enough, the invitations will slowly fade away. If you want to maintain friendships, then you can be honest with those you feel close to. Learn to differentiate between those who genuinely care for you and others who treat you like a doormat.

Trust and honesty

Trust and honesty are two traits that empaths look for in everyone they meet. Your intuition essentially makes you a human lie detector. Even if the other person is trying to conceal his real intentions, you will get to know about it. Therefore, trust and honesty matter a lot for an empath and rightly so.

Exercises

In this section, you'll learn about certain simple exercises you can perform daily to protect yourself from narcissists and other energy vampires.

Empaths feel everything, and it soon becomes quite overwhelming.

Shielding

Shield yourself as the quickest ways in which you can protect yourself is why shielding. Empaths usually use this technique for blocking out any toxic energy that's present around them while allowing positive energy to flow freely. You can use this exercise whenever you want. If you feel like you're in the presence of an energy vampire for filing a situation that's draining you out, then use your energy shield. In fact, if you're dealing with narcissistic parents or siblings, you can still use this shielding visualization.

To practice this exercise, start by taking a couple of deep and long breaths. As you breathe in and breathe out and start visualizing a beautiful shield of white and pleasant light is surrounding your body. It is forming a protective layer around you.

As you keep breathing in and breathing out, this protective shield is becoming stronger and stronger. This shield of positivity protects you from all sorts of toxic and intrusive energies. By being present within this shield, you feel happy and re-energized. You can call upon this shield whenever you want a little extra help dealing with an energy vampire.

Avoid empathy overload

If you're trying to prevent empathy overload, then the simplest way of distressing is by using lavender essential oil. This oil tends to have a calming effect and is often used as a stress buster. Mix this oil with your regular moisturizer and use it to massage your temples. Rub it in slowly, and you can feel your mind become, and more relaxed.

Another simple way to avoid empathy overload is by learning how to say "no." The word no is a complete sentence all by itself. You don't owe anyone any explanations, and you don't have to try to please everyone else. Not just explanations, you don't owe anyone anything. Remember that you're not indebted to anyone, and you are free to live the kind of life you desire. You are free to do whatever you want. Keep reminding yourself of all this. Learn how to say no and learn to stick by your nose. As an empath, saying no might not be the easiest thing in the world, but it is much required for your wellbeing.

Protection meditation

Revisit all the steps you followed in the shielding visualization exercise. Now, it is time to take it a step ahead and make it more powerful. Once you have established a protective shield around you, call upon the spirit of the jaguar to protect you. The jaguar is believed to be a fierce and loving guard who will keep toxic people and energy away from you. Call upon this protective spirit and try to visualize this powerful and majestic creature patrolling your energy field. The way a jaguar would protect her young cubs, the jaguar is now protecting you. Try to make this visualization as clear as you can. Try to imagine what the jaguar looks like and concentrate on the way she moves around you. Once you feel safe and secure, it is time to express your gratitude to the jaguar. I usually use this exercise whenever I feel like I'm in a toxic environment I cannot immediately escape from. Feel free to call upon the spirit of the jaguar to protect you whenever you want.

Chapter 6: Thriving As An Empath At Work

Unhealthy Dynamics Empaths Need Be Aware Of

Revealing too much about themselves

Empaths must be aware of any unhealthy dynamic that exists in the workplace. You tend to spend a significant portion of your time and attention at your place of work. Therefore, it is quintessential that you work in a healthy environment. It is important to share information about yourself, performing healthy relationships. However, you must be mindful of the information you share. If you aren't careful, you might end up revealing a little too much about yourself. If you do this, you are essentially making yourself the target of any narcissistic colleagues you have.

Forming alliances with needy colleagues

As an empath, you will be drawn to any pain or suffering you see around you. It is a natural instinct to try and help such people who are in need. However, if you spend too much time with such people, you will eventually end up feeling quite miserable and tired. It is okay to help others, but it is not okay to form strong alliances with needy colleagues. For instance, it is okay if you are helping out a colleague when he is sick and is unable to complete his work on time. However, it is not okay to help someone who is merely trying to shrug all the responsibility and make others do the work for them. Don't help a colleague with his work because he doesn't feel like working or because he wants to go home early. Be mindful of all those you help and when you help them. After all, you are in a professional environment where everyone has certain roles to play. You're not responsible for everyone, and you don't have to do other's work.

Always saying yes

Saying "no" is not easy, and a lot of people struggle with this. I know I used to struggle with the same thing until a couple of years ago. By learning to say no, you are not only standing up for yourself but are also respecting the boundaries you have set for yourself. Your inability to say "no" will be easily exploited by manipulative people. You must understand what your professional boundaries are and must adhere to such boundaries. Don't do anything to cross your personal limits, and don't give anyone else the liberty to do the same to you. If you cannot do something, or if you feel like you are being taken undue advantage of, then it is time to say "no." If you don't, then within no time, you will notice that you are on the receiving end of job dumping. This is a tactic used by manipulative people to get others to do their work for them.

Well, why should you do something, which isn't included in your job description? You don't have to agree with things others say because you don't want to displease them. Stop worrying about conflicts. Yes, I agree that as an empath, you wouldn't want to indulge in any unnecessary conflicts. However, at times, it is important to put your foot down and say no so that others don't take you for granted.

Self-sacrifice

Empaths often see themselves and others. They believe that others also think and feel the way they do. Well, this is kind of naive, and this is not the way things progress in the real world. It is okay to make a couple of sacrifices every now and then, especially if it is for a good cause. However, don't lull yourself into believing that by working hard, you will be rewarded by others. For instance, if you do your work along with the work that's assigned to your coworker, don't be under the misimpression that you will be rewarded for all the work you did. You will be rewarded for your work, while your coworker will also be rewarded for your work that he passed off as his own. If you are working in a healthy work environment, then you will get the recognition you deserve. Be careful about all the people you help, and don't unnecessarily make a martyr of yourself.

Playing it too safe

I am sure that after going through all these different aspects discussed up until now, you will be tempted to play safely at work. Remember a simple rule whenever you approach anything in life- there is no reward without risk. If you don't take any risks and play it too safe, then don't expect any major rewards. Having said that, you must be mindful of the risks you assume. Don't be foolhardy and never bite more than you can swallow. Evaluate your potential of withstanding risks and take calculated risks.

Why Empath Get So Tired

As an empath, spending time in public is quite tiring. So, if you have to spend about 8 hours daily at your workplace, it will become extremely tiring for you.

Constant inner-contraction

Dealing with emotions that aren't your own is never easy. Since you can't help by feel what others feel, it is quite important that you maintain certain boundaries at work. The workplace is usually full of tensions, and this can make you feel extremely fatigued and drained out. Dealing with conflicts, tension, and stress is always unpleasant. However, it is way worse for an empath. Receiving any negative emotions from others and being sucked into workplace drama can make you feel extremely frustrated and stressed out.

Unfulfilling jobs lead to fatigue

How do you feel the moment you get home after work? Most of us tend to feel rather relieved and happy to be back in our safe spots. Well, I am not talking about this feeling. What do you feel when you talk about your work with others? Does talking about your work make you feel happy and excited? Or does it fill you with an unexplainable feeling of dread? If all that you feel is fatigue whenever you think about your work, then maybe you are stuck in an unfulfilling job. Don't worry, because there is some good news here. The good news is that this is an indication for you to leave!

Deal with manipulative people at work

If you are like me, I am sure that it takes every ounce of energy you have to spend any length of time in a place that is visually stimulating and extremely noisy. Quite certain that working for someone who is explicitly self-centered, self-absorbed, and conceited will make for an unforgettable experience. It is quite difficult to work for someone when all that person does is take credit for everything that you do and blame you when something goes wrong. A person who is manipulative often spends a lot of his time thinking about ways in which he can gain more power and influence over others. If you're dealing with a narcissistic boss, then it is quite likely that he often over exaggerates his self-importance. Perhaps the worst thing about working for a narcissist is that he would never accept that here's the problem. In fact, he might have a couple of employees you would use a scapegoat whenever something goes wrong. Whenever his fancy strikes, he might just randomly choose another employee to take the fall for his wrong actions.

If you are working for a narcissist, then you have two options you can either quit your job or learn how to deal with the narcissist. If you cannot lose your job and want to stay at your existing place of work, then you must learn how to deal with your boss. In this section, you will learn about different practical tips you can use to deal with such a person with our allowing him to drive you crazy. As an empath, you are a natural magnet to a narcissist. To deal with him, you must first try to understand him. The chance that narcissists will change for the better is quite small and working with them will never become easy. However, you can make it more manageable.

Deal With Toxic People

How often did I wish I had the power to pick my coworkers. Well, the reality of life is that you don't get to choose who your coworkers and your bosses are. This inability to choose them does have a significant impact on an empath's work life. Whenever a boss, coworker, or even a client becomes especially toxic, it can be quite challenging to work. Being exposed to negative, unstable, or even chaotic people for prolonged periods will have a negative effect on your emotions. The amount of stress you feel because of this anxiety you experience will certainly harm your physical and mental wellbeing. However, the good news is that there are a couple of things you can do to make sure that you are coping with all the toxic people you interact with at work.

Control yourself

All empaths always see the good in others. It can be rather tempting to spend all your time and energy hoping that your manager or maybe even your coworkers will become more supportive and will stop targeting you. All this is wishful thinking, and all it does is wasted time and energy. Instead of trying to control others, direct your energy towards controlling yourself. You certainly cannot control others, but you can control the way you react and respond to them. Regardless of whether you decide to keep quiet or speak up, it is important that you channel your energy into taking positive action.

Accepting responsibility

I am sure you are good at accepting your responsibility whenever things go wrong. It is okay to do this. However, it is not okay to take responsibility for the way others feel. You are not responsible for all this. The only thing you are responsible for is the way you feel. If someone is making you feel bad about something, then it is because you have given them the power to make you feel bad about it. You can always put your foot down, and it is time you realize that you're the only one who can regulate this. If you keep allowing others to violate your personal space, then don't complain about it later. After all, you have given them the liberty to do this.

Care for yourself

Whenever you're dealing with a toxic individual, you must deal with them using all the energy you have within you. When you are feeling confident and positive, it becomes easier to deal with any toxicity that comes your way. Therefore, it is quintessential that you start taking steps to indulge in the necessary self-care. The better you feel, the easier it is to deal with all those people who come your way. If you are feeling low on energy and rather vulnerable, then you are making yourself an easy target for all toxic people.

Physical distance

As discussed in the previous chapter, emotional contagion is quite real. I mean, emotions are contagious and that too literally. Being around a person who is unstable and miserable can rob you of the wrong way. So, whenever possible, try to distance yourself from such people physically. If you can, avoid interacting with those people altogether. It will certainly make your job a lot easier when you can limit your exposure to such negativity.

Redirecting yourself

Toxic people love to play mind games with their victims. Therefore, it is not surprising that they can easily get into the head of an empath. So, I urge you to remember this and redirect yourself toward everything that is positive. Think about all the things that you love about your job and concentrate on those things. Forget about all the negativity around you, and you will feel better about yourself and your work.

Draw the line

If you feel like your boundaries are not being respected and that they're being violated regularly, and you are unable to control the situation regardless of what you do, then you can think about filing a complaint. Don't make it personal and keep things strictly professional. Describe whatever is going on as directly and clearly as you possibly can. Being harassed by a toxic person is never pleasant, and reporting it is well within your rights. When it comes to protecting yourself, whether it is physically or mentally, it is okay to put your foot down. However, you must know when you are supposed to draw this line.

You are better

Toxic people seldom have the emotional intelligence that an empath has. Therefore, you cannot expect them to behave the way you do. Don't allow yourself to be bogged down by petty and irrational behavior. You are much better than this. This becomes quite easy to do, especially when the behavior exhibited by the toxic person starts to become quite irrational. Concentrate on maintaining your emotional and intellectual integrity instead of worrying about the way the toxic person is behaving. As long as this person's behavior doesn't cause you any harm, ignore it. Most of these people often do these things to get attention. They love being in the limelight, and when they don't get the attention they desire, they start behaving like unruly children. So, the best thing you can do in such a situation is to ignore them and not give them the attention they want.

Come up with solutions

It is quite easy to get bogged down mentally, especially when you're thinking about all the problems you're faced with. Instead of worrying about how annoying the problems are, start concentrating on the solutions. Think about ways in which you can deal with them at work. You cannot change the way they behave, but you can certainly control your reactions. Train yourself to concentrate on the answers instead of all the questions you're facing. By dwelling on all the problems you face, you're not doing yourself any favors. In fact, you're merely tiring yourself out.

Out of sight out of mind

When the day ends, and it is time to get back home, forget about all the toxic people you deal with. Make sure that you separate your professional life from your personal life. Don't allow the toxic person to stay in your head once you back in the comfort of your home. You already spent enough of your time and energy dealing with such people. You don't need them following you to your safe haven. Don't obsess over all the instances that irritated you throughout the day. Forget about all the unnecessary things and worries. You can always deal with these things the next time you set foot at work. Enjoy the peace you have right now and don't allow anyone else to take this away from you.

Realization

Don't be under any misconceptions that the toxic person you're dealing with can feel any compassion towards you. Toxic individuals cannot feel any compassion whatsoever. Thy certainly love it when they are getting attention and compassion from others, but they cannot reciprocate these feelings. This kind of people always shift the blame onto others, especially when things don't go as they're supposed to. Then ever think that they are the problem and that they are the ones who are making all the mistakes. This is one of the major problems you will have to tackle while dealing with toxic individuals. You probably think that you'll be able to reason with them or even appeal to the compassionate side. If this is rotating, then I am sorry to burst your bubble because you're sadly mistaken. The toxic person you're dealing with is not worried about how his acts affect you. In fact, all that they would be worried about is themselves.

As long as something doesn't affect them directly, it is not their concern. So, stop wasting your time and energy trying to elicit some compassion from a being who is incapable of feeling any compassion.

Being mentally strong

There is nothing as terrible as self-pity. Mentally strong people wouldn't waste their time or energy by feeling sorry for themselves or by wallowing in self-pity. Instead, they take responsibility for their actions and try to understand how they can improve the situation instead of thinking about how unfair the circumstances are or how poorly others have treated them. They would never allow someone else to push their buttons or control their actions. They wouldn't let someone else boss over them or make them feel terrible. A mentally strong person knows that they are in control of their emotions, and they can choose the way in which they want to respond in a given situation. This is exactly what you are supposed to do. Don't allow others to control you and start developing the mental strength required to deal with the realities of life. Who doesn't have negative feelings? A mentally strong person knows that there is no point in encouraging negative thoughts, and such a person would try to reframe all their negative thoughts into positive ones. Instead of getting discouraged by the negative thoughts, they would think of a way in which they can make it positive. They consciously try to change the pessimistic dialogue in their head to something positive that will encourage them to work harder. Whenever they feel low, they give themselves a pep talk. So, start being your own cheerleader and take control of your life. You can control the thoughts you think and the emotions you feel. You can control the way you respond to any situation. Start concentrating on these things instead of worrying about all the things you cannot do.

It is quite easy to get distracted by different thoughts and things. Did you ever start working and get distracted by something that's entirely different? Not everything is essential, and you indeed don't have to exert the same mental energy and focus. A mentally strong person is capable of prioritizing and knows the importance of making proper use of their mental energy to accomplish their goals.

Create Sacred Space at Work

Establish a successful and fulfilling professional life; it is quintessential that you are happy at your workplace, and the environment you are working on is conducive to productivity. If your place of work matches your temperament and energizes you, then you'll be inspired to better and work more. Apart from this, it also improves your creativity while increasing your passion and dedication towards your work. That said, if the environment to work on is negative, then it could suck the life right out of you. In fact, it can also trigger a variety of emotional and physical symptoms because of all the stress you deal with. Negativity festers negativity and positivity fester positivity. For an empath, working in a negative environment is never desirable. Not getting sufficient time to rest and being overburdened emotionally can wreak havoc on your health - physical as well as mental. When presented with the right kind of work and the right environment, empaths and sensitive people will thrive and flourish.

Since most of us spend a lot of our waking hours at work, it is quintessential to ensure that you feel at ease while at your workplace. There are three different factors that are important for ensuring your comfort level at work. These three factors include the meaning you derive from your job, the energy of the environment you work on, and the energy of all those people you work with. To evaluate the importance of these three major factors, it is time for a little self-introspection. Find a quiet place, get rid of all distractions, and start thinking about your work. You must think about it rationally and don't allow any emotions to guide your decisions and opinions.

The first thing you must address is the meaning you derive from your job. Since you spend about 6 to 8 hours actively engaged in your work, it is important that it adds some value or meaning to your life. If the work you're doing doesn't add any value to your life, then you will obviously feel like you're being overburdened. When you enjoy the work you do, and it adds value to your life, your inclination to work better and work more will increase.

The next aspect of your work you must evaluate is the environment to work on. How would you describe your workplace environment? Does it seem positive or negative to you? As an empath, you can easily answer this question. All that you need to do is be mindful of the energy you are surrounded by, and you will have your answer.

How do you feel when you step into your office? Are you filled with positivity, or does it feel like you are staring into an endless black hole? If you feel motivated and uplifted the moment you enter your workspace, then you're working in a healthy environment. If you don't feel these emotions, then you need to make some changes to your workplace environment.

The third factor you must evaluate the people you work with. As an empath, you are quite sensitive to the energies of those around you. So, if you're surrounded by negative people, you will feel quite low on energy. On the other hand, if you're surrounded by happy, upbeat, and motivated people, you will feel the same. If you think that you are surrounded by negative people, then it is time that you come up with different ways in which you can work on rectifying the situation.

Spend some time and think about all these three factors and start coming up with a plan about how you can improve your current situation. Every space tends to have a specific subtle energy of its own. Some places might be quite uplifting, while others are not. My personal suggestion is that you tried to understand the energy of your workplace and take steps to change it such that it feels right to you. In this section, you will learn about three simple ways in which you can create a sacred space for yourself at work.

Energetic boundaries

Setting energetic boundaries is very important to create an uplifting work environment. If you have an office to yourself, it becomes quite easy to set energetic boundaries. However, if all that you have is a cubicle or an open space in a chaotic work environment, then how do you set these energetic boundaries? Well, the simplest thing you can do is to place pictures of your loved ones along with some plants around the outer edge of your desk. Apart from this, you can also use other protective items like the statue of Buddha, crystals, protective stone, or even sacred beads. You are essentially aligning your desk with all items that act as amulets.

If you're working in an environment that is rather chaotic, then investing in a good pair of noise-canceling earbuds or headphones is a good idea. It helps get rid of any unnecessary noises and sounds. An empath can be easily overstimulated in a chaotic environment. By limiting the stimulation of your sensory organs, you can make working in a chaotic environment easy for yourself. Apart from this, make sure that you take regular breaks. Don't stay stuck to your desk all the time. Move around a little. Whenever you want, take a break and go outside for a walk. Spend a couple of minutes in nature, and you will feel better.

Purify the energy

Once your limits are set, it is time to purify the energy that's present in your workspace. A nonintrusive way to purify the energy around you is to spirits rose water in the room. Burning sage is a great idea, when at home. But I wouldn't recommend burning sage at your workplace. It may not only cause disturbance to other employees but might also set off the fire alarms. After all, whatever you are trying to do must never be a source of discomfort for others. You can also use the power of meditation to remove any negative or stagnant energy from your workspace. Spend some time and meditate by sending out positive energy and thoughts into your workspace. You can also optimize the positive energy in space through the placement of certain objects like furniture, plants, or even mirrors.

Coping mechanism

The way you feel and the way you work is influenced by all those people you work with. When you're surrounded by negative people, you will experience negative energy. Likewise, when you're surrounded by happy and positive people, you'll be filled with positive energy. The comfort you feel in your workspace essentially depends on the energy given out by your coworkers, colleagues, and bosses. A highly sensitive person usually has a very low threshold for noise, conflict, feuds, backstabbing, and office politics. All the drama that is related to work, which might seem like a minor disturbance to others, will feel quite tiring for an empath. Working in such an environment will only make you feel anxious and stressed out. You'll come across different types of energy vampires while at your workplace. You might run into narcissists, passive-aggressive people, drama queens, or even those who talk incessantly. Learning to deal with all these people is quite important if you want to work. It is highly unlikely that you'll find workspace, which is filled only with empaths. You will certainly find like-minded people wherever you work, but you will also find those who will drain you of your energy. Therefore, I suggest that you come up with a couple of coping mechanisms to ensure that your energy is not negatively affected.

A simple strategy that I use to cope with such people at work is that I try putting as much physical distance between myself and the other person. Whenever possible, I avoid talking to the other person or even interacting with them. Apart from this, I keep things strictly professional and avoid talking about any personal things.

Certainly, it is not possible to control every aspect of your work environment, but you do have the power to shift the energy present within your immediate surroundings. By focusing on creating a safe space for yourself, you can avoid all the confusion and chaos prevalent in your workspace. Once you do this, you will start to feel more relaxed and pleasant. When you feel safe and secure in your environment, your ability to work will improve. By following these steps, you can improve the level of positivity in your office. Not just that, but it will also help improve your overall productivity.

Exercises

The best way to take stock of all the different activities that nourish and harm you is by journalizing.

Once you are home after work or maybe before you go to sleep at night, set some time aside for journalizing. You must reflect upon the day you had, all the tasks you performed, the things you did well, the changes you would want to make, and so on. You are essentially giving yourself a quick recap of the day you had.

After this, it is time to start making a list of all the different activities and tasks you performed during the day. Make a note of everything, even the ones which seem trivial and silly to you. Everything you do takes a little bit of your energy.

Once the list is ready, it is time for some honest self-evaluation. It is time to rate all these events on a scale of one to five. With one being completely drained of energy and five being extremely energizing. For instance, dealing with a manipulative manager might make you feel completely drained and out of your energy while spending time on an activity you enjoy will be extremely energizing.

Once this list is ready and each task has an energy meter next to it, it is time to come up with ways in which you can limit or remove these exhausting tasks. It might not always be possible to eliminate certain tasks like conversing with a manipulative boss or manager, but you can certainly limit such interactions.

While doing this, you must also come up with ways in which you can create more time to indulge in activities that make you feel energized and happy.

After you do all this, it is time to start incorporating these ideas. After all, a plan that is never implemented doesn't amount to anything. Start doing things you are good at and start delegating tasks that can be delegated whenever you start running low on energy. Don't try to do everything by yourself and learn how to delegate tasks. Also, limit your interactions with toxic colleagues.

Chapter 7: On Healthy Relationships And Avoiding The Narcissistic Downward Spiral

Things Empaths Need in a Relationship

In this section, you will learn about the different elements of a successful and healthy relationship. Only when all these elements exist in your relationship will it thrive and flourish.

The pace matters

The pace at which you want your relationship to progress is quite important. The pace you decide upon must be something that you and your partner are both comfortable. At times, when you start dating someone, it might feel like you're spending every waking moment of your day with them. You probably do this because you want to, and that's brilliant. However, make sure that you don't feel like you are rushing into a relationship or are being forced to do something you normally wouldn't have done. The relationship must not be a source of stress, and it must move at a comfortable pace.

Trust

Trust is one of the cornerstones of a healthy relationship. If the trust doesn't exist, then the relationship will not survive. You must not only have faith in your partner that he will not hurt you, but you must also have faith that he will not do anything to ruin the relationship. There needs to be mutual trust. There needs to be a shared trust that neither you nor your partner would do anything to violate each other's trust. Apart from this, also make sure that you are not necessarily going out of your way to earning your partner's trust.

Independence

Having personal space and independence in the relationship is quintessential. This is extremely important for every relationship and even more so for empaths. For instance, your partner must be fine with the fact that you do have a life outside of the relationship and must not behave like you're attached at the hip or demand that he knows every little detail about your life. Sharing is important, but so is personal space. As long as you don't violate each other's trust, then having personal space is good for the health of the relationship. Not just the relationship, but even for your mental health. You obviously need some time alone to recharge your drained batteries.

Honesty

Trust and honesty go hand-in-hand. As an empath, you are attuned to the emotions of those around you. This means, if your partner is dishonest, you'll get about it immediately. Therefore, it is important that there exists honesty. In a healthy relationship, you must be able to talk to your partner about any topic under the sun without worrying about being judged. If open, honest communication doesn't exist in a relationship, then the relationship is doomed. You must not have to hide the way you feel or the opinions you have merely because you're worried about upsetting your partner. Likewise, even your partner must be honest with you.

Respect

Respect is present in a relationship when you and your partner value each other's opinions, beliefs, and individuality. Simple instances of respect include supporting each other, complementing each other, and not overstepping once boundaries. Respect can also be shown by sticking up for each other.

Compassion

As an empath, you are highly compassionate towards a partner. However, compassion must be a two-way street. You cannot keep giving, and your partner cannot be on the receiving end all the time. Even an empath needs a little compassion from time to time. Your partner must express feelings of care and concern toward you. If you are in a healthy relationship, then your partner will be understanding, supportive, and kind to you. Regardless of what you're going through, your partner will always give you the support you require to keep going.

Equality

A healthy relationship exists only once the playing field is equal. You and your partner must treat each other as equals. The relationship must not feel like one of the partners has more say than the other or that one partner put in more effort than the other. For instance, you can say quality exists in a relationship when any decision that affects both of you is decided together as a team instead of one person calling all the shots.

Responsibility

Empaths are always willing to take responsibility for their actions. However, you and your partner must both be responsible for your own actions and the words you say. You must not put the blame on each other and must own up to your acts. For instance, you must not allow your partner to take out his frustration out on you because he is upset for some reason. That kind of behavior isn't acceptable. At the same time, you shouldn't have to take responsibility for your partner's mistakes.

Communication

A sign of a healthy relationship is one you are free to talk to your partner about everything, regardless of whether it is good or bad. You can do this only when you know your partner will listen to you and is open to discussing the topics you wish to talk about. If you feel like your partner is too judgmental of your opinions, then healthy communication will be missing in your relationship.

Downward Spiral with Narcissists

A relationship shared between an empath, and a narcissist can never be healthy, and it is always toxic. Empaths and narcissists are the two extreme ends on the spectrum of empathy. Opposites attract, and this is quite true. This rule has plenty of potentials when you're trying to broaden your horizons. However, it also means that certain people would be drawn to your energy for all the wrong reasons. For instance, narcissists are often attracted to those who will be useful to them. So, it is quite obvious that empaths make perfect targets for them. Narcissists are quite the opposite of empaths. All those individuals who have a narcissistic personality disorder have no empathy whatsoever, and they thrive on attention. Empaths are quite sensitive and are in tune with the emotions of those around them. Empaths are like emotional sponges who keep absorbing feelings and emotions from others rather easily. This makes them quite appealing to narcissists because, the empath is someone who will always fulfill the needs without expecting anything in return. This kind of toxic attraction is a recipe for disaster for an empath.

When a narcissist sees an empath, all he sees as a person who's loving and nurturing. Or a person who will be quite devoted to him and will listen to him regardless of what he says. It is quite sad that empaths are often attracted to narcissists, and usually, they are attracted to the facade the narcissists put up. Narcissists can be quite charming and even giving initially. All this slowly fades away when you stop doing things the way they want and start showing independence. When a narcissist is trying to gain an empath's trust, he will seem quite charming, intelligent, caring, and nurturing. I know all this from personal experience. One of my first relationships and life was with a narcissist. It wasn't until later I realized that I was dealing with a narcissist. In the initial stages of a relationship, everything is peachy, and all was going well. It felt like I finally found my one true love, and I was quite happy. However, all this was not meant to last. I couldn't see all the red flags presented by my narcissistic partner. In fact, in hindsight, it is fair to say that I did see certain red flags, but I chose to ignore them. I kept giving and giving until I could no longer give anything more. If only I trusted my intuition and relied on my cart, I could have avoided all this drama in my life.

Co-dependency

Empaths thrive when there is harmony around them, whereas a narcissist thrives when there is chaos. The kind of chaos that narcissists enjoyed is never desirable for an average human being, let alone someone who is highly sensitive. They love pulling out of people's strengths and make them their puppets. Narcissists can easily manipulate empath by stringing along while providing intermittent hope. They usually incorporate things like compliments and kindness into the usual behavior. This often makes the victim believes that if they behave in the proper manner, they will be loved. A relationship with a narcissist is often one-sided. As long as the narcissist gets what he wants, he wouldn't care about others.

Empaths have an inherent tendency to understand that all humans have flaws. In fact, they are willing to be quite patient if it means helping someone else. And if someone else happens to be a romantic partner, then an empath will never hesitate to offer any help. If a narcissist says, "I know are not perfect, and I'm trying to change," an empath should give him the benefit of the doubt. This kind of relationship is quite toxic for the empath. A narcissist is incapable of changing. The more you believe and the more chances you give him, the more will he exploit you. Narcissists usually use psychological tactics for reeling the victims back into that trap. When it comes to using this with empaths, it is quite effective. Knowingly or unknowingly, you are only fueling the cycle of unhealthy codependency. Empaths have a strong urge to make others happy, and a narcissist knows this quite well.

Trauma bonding

A trauma bond is often created between the abuser and the victim because of the push and pull, which exists in a narcissistic relationship. This trauma bond makes the empaths feel like it is almost impossible to let go of the relationship, regardless of the damage it causes. One of the drawbacks of empathy is that it comes with a lot of self-awareness. As an empath, I'm pretty sure that you tend to look at yourself and your faults. In fact, I'm sure that you often see your flaws and keep apologizing for them. This wonderful ability of yours is often exploited by a narcissist. All it does is strengthen the trauma bond is forming. It creates a vicious cycle for empaths who have formed a trauma bond because they start to look at themselves, the things they need to change about themselves, and all that they have to do differently. They accept the character flaws and work hard on making amends. Unfortunately, this is the perfect setup for a narcissist. It can be quite difficult to understand the fact that you are stuck in a narcissistic relationship. They might have been plenty of red flags you have seen had you been more attentive. If you want to protect yourself from narcissistic abuse, then it is high time that you understand you are responsible for yourself. You are responsible for your own personal growth and that you are not responsible for others.

Over identification

Being compassionate towards someone is quite different from over-identifying with him. A lot of people don't understand this distinction. Since you are a highly sensitive empath, you might feel like you're inclined to feel sorry for others. In this process, you end up losing yourself in the relationship or stop taking care of yourself. Never try to over-identify with your partner, especially if the set partner is a narcissist or an energy vampire. There is nothing wrong with feeling compassionate towards others, but when you start over identifying yourself with others, this is when it all goes wrong. Over-identification is the process of identifying yourself to an excessive degree with someone else, to the extent that it is harmful to your wellbeing.

Here's a simple example that will give you a better understanding of what over identification looks like. For instance, let us assume that you and your narcissistic partner were first drawn to each other because of shared trauma. Maybe you both experienced childhood trauma or you were children of a bad marriage. This might have been the common bond between you two, at least initially. Whenever your narcissistic partner does something, you often write it down to his childhood trauma or suffering. Even when you know what he is doing is wrong, you choose to overlook it because you think it is because of his faulty upbringing. It comes to a stage where you feel a little too much empathy and compassion for him regardless of the harm he inflicts on you. This relationship is toxic from the get-go. It is okay to bond over a traumatic event, but that must not be the defining factor of a relationship. Poor behavior is never justified. It is not okay to keep giving someone chances, again and again, only to be let down. Understand this and come to terms with the fact that you are stuck in a toxic relationship. Stop over-identifying yourself with your narcissistic partner.

Highly giving, forgiving

Since you are an empath, it is in your nature to be quite forgiving and extremely giving. You understand that humans are flawed, and that means they will make mistakes. If someone makes a mistake, they do deserve a second chance, don't they? Well, it is okay to give someone a second chance and give them an opportunity to make amends. However, it is not okay to keep giving someone chances again and again, with the end result being disappointed every single time. If you keep giving and then giving some more in a relationship without getting anything in return, it is highly one-sided. A narcissist thrives in such a relationship, whereas an empath slowly loses the sense of self. It is okay to be trusting and forgiving, but it is not okay to be gullible. It is not okay to let others take undue advantage of you and take you for granted. You must remind yourself that you are not an emotional doormat that your narcissistic partner can walk all over. You must stand for yourself. A relationship cannot exist at first when one partner keeps giving, and the other one only keeps receiving. There must be give and take in a healthy relationship. If either of these aspects is missing, then you're stuck in a harmful relationship. The sooner you realize this, the better it is for your overall wellbeing. Start listening to your intuition and follow the little voice in your head.

When you keep forgiving a narcissistic partner all the time, then the narcissist will take this for granted. In fact, he will merely do things to test the limits to which he can push you. Once he understands that he will always be forgiven, there is nothing that will stop him from harming you. For instance, let us assume that you caught your partner cheating on you. You confronted him, and he apologized to you for the same. He apologized and promised that he would make amends and not repeat in such undesirable behavior ever again. However, a couple of weeks down the line, you notice that he is unfaithful once again. If you forgive him even after this, then he will come to the conclusion that you can be pushed around. And that you will always be there for him regardless of all that he does. It only gives him the motivation to act more poorly.

Natural nurturer

Empaths have an inherent desire to nurture others. Empaths thrive when those around them are happy. A narcissist thrives on attention. Empaths can feel the pain that others are in. Once they feel this pain, then they will try to do everything they can to help others feel better and leave them of their suffering. It is quite normal to want to reach out to all those people who are hurt and try to make them feel better. However, an empath does this more than what can be considered to be desirable. They tend to absorb all the pain and the helplessness of the partners. In the end, all this task is to make you feel quite upset and drained out. A narcissist knows this and will use it to his advantage. Not only will he exploit your empathic nature, but he will do so without batting an eyelid. If it means he can get his way and his needs will be met, he doesn't care about the costs involved. The more you give, the more will the narcissist expect. You don't have to take care of him all the time. A narcissist might throw a tantrum when he doesn't get his way, and you might even feel guilty for denying him something. Well, for your own wellbeing, it is a good idea to understand the things that are okay and not okay with you. Make a list of your personal boundaries and start implementing them. If your narcissistic partner cannot respect your boundaries, then it is a clear sign that you are in a toxic relationship.

After all, when you are with a person who truly loves you and will stand by you, then he will respect your boundaries.

Fight for the underdog

Because of your empathetic nature, it is quite normal that you tend to feel immense compassion towards all those who are victims of social inequality and injustice. This is one of the reasons why empaths tend to root for the underdog. As an empath, it is your natural tendency to support the site, which you think needs more help. So, if you view your narcissistic partner as being an underdog, it is quite likely that you'll be drawn to him. For instance, if you know that your narcissistic partner suffered some form of abuse in his childhood, then you will feel compassionate toward him. This means you might even be willing to turn a blind eye toward all the undesirable behaviors he indulges in. Well, it is time to change this perspective of yours. It is okay to fight for the underdog. However, it is not okay to ignore poor behavior. So, choose your battles wisely and always make sure that you are on the right side.

How to avoid a narcissist

All empaths are natural healers. You all have an inherent desire to help others because they tend to understand what others are going through. Because of all this, they always try to see the good in others and believe that everyone is good. As naive as it sounds, they often believe that others also think and feel the way they do. Well, I'm sorry to burst your bubble, but you are in for massive disappointment excesses how you go about life. It is high time we realize that not everyone is willing to take responsibility for their actions. If you know you made a mistake, you might be the first one to offer an apology and make amends. Not everyone is like you, and not everyone likes apologizing or accepting the responsibility for the mistakes they made. Remind yourself that not everyone will share your beliefs and that the motives for behaving the way they do are probably beyond your comprehension.

An empath is not good at understanding that some people will never take responsibility for their actions because they feel like they are not wrong, and because of this, do nothing to apologize for. All such people only care about what they want and don't really care if anyone gets hurt in this process. That said, it is not unfair to say that everyone you come across in your life would be a narcissist or manipulative person, but people can be toxic in ways that are less obvious than this. You are stuck in an abusive relationship if you get involved with someone who is not good for your wellbeing.

Even if you refuse to believe this, I must remind you that empaths naturally attract toxic people because of their empathic nature. An empath ability to take responsibility for not just their actions, but also for those around them, makes them attractive targets for a narcissist. If anything does go wrong, then be prepared to be blamed for everything that went wrong. If you are dealing with a narcissist, this is bound to happen at one point or the other. In fact, don't be surprised if the narcissist allows you to take the fall for their misdeeds and happily shift all the blame onto your head and walk away unscathed.

What would you do when you see that someone is angry or hurt? Well, you might start thinking about ways in which you can help them. You probably do this because you're disillusioned by the belief that it was your own actions that earned you your partner's unpleasant reaction. So, by doing this, you are effectively freeing your narcissistic partner from taking any responsibility for his actions. The toxic person will be more than happy to allow you to take the fall for him because it means he is not responsible for whatever that went wrong. To avoid all this, you must start practicing the different exercises discussed in the next section.

Exercises

Here are a couple of simple exercises you can use to ensure your wellbeing in any relationship.

People are scared of expressing their fears. After all, expressing one's fears not only brings about feelings of vulnerability but also means acceptance of one's flaws. This isn't an easy thing to do. However, if you want to establish healthy relationships in your life, then it is quintessential that you work on addressing your fears. I believe we all struggle with this because of unfair societal conditioning. We have all been repeatedly told that being vulnerable is not a good thing and is often viewed as a sign of weakness. This, in turn, means that a lot of people are usually pretending to be someone they aren't. It is okay to be vulnerable. When you share your vulnerabilities with a partner who loves and respects you, it paves the way for a healthy and mutually satisfying relationship. While doing this, be mindful of all those people you let in. Don't make your vulnerabilities known to a narcissist or other toxic people.

Before you can share your fears, you must become aware of your fears. It is time for a little self-introspection. Sit down and start making a list of all the fears you have about expressing yourself. It doesn't matter whether the things you are making a note of are rational or not. Fears are seldom rational, so don't go into explaining anything, at least not yet. Merely make a list of your fears.

Once you do this, it is time to establish certain boundaries for yourself. These boundaries you make a note of are your personal limits. Any behavior that breaks these boundaries is undesirable. It essentially shows how far you are willing to go to make a relationship work. You must not only establish these boundaries but must also enforce them. You must also set the consequences for when these limits are ignored. For instance, if dishonesty is a deal-breaker for you, then make a note of it. If you notice that your partner is being dishonest and is refusing to change his ways, then it is time to cut your losses and sever all ties with him. These boundaries you establish for yourself will act as a guiding force in your relationship. They will also help ensure that you are staying true to yourself and aren't doing anything that you usually believed to be unreasonable.

Now, it is time to make a list of all the things you must express in your relationship. Once you have a list of things, start doing at least one of these things daily. For instance, if you want your partner to take an active part in household chores, but never told him about this because you were worried about his reaction. Well, there is no time like the present to have this conversation. If you are in a healthy relationship, then this conversation will not be turbulent.

It is time for a little self-introspection once again. Spend some time and start making a list of all the positive qualities you wish you had. It could be something as simple as the ability to be more confident or even assertive and strong. You will need to take a long and hard look at yourself and come to terms with the fact that there are some flaws you must work on improving. It is okay to have certain weaknesses. However, it is not okay to allow these weaknesses to stand in between you and the happiness you desire. Once you accept and acknowledge your weaknesses, you can start working on improving them. Now, it is time to select a role model for yourself. There must be someone you see or know who exhibits all the traits you wish you had. This person might be someone you know, like your family member, a friend, or maybe even someone you never met, like an actor! It doesn't matter who this person is, as long as he or she exhibits all the behaviors you desire.

The final step is to overcome any reservations you have about expressing yourself. If you are not sure how to go about doing this, then here is a simple question you must ask yourself.

What would (the above-mentioned person) do if she were in the same situation as me?

Think about the way the said person would behave and start imagining yourself as that person you just described. Notice the way you feel. I use this technique whenever I struggle with something in life. At times, imagining a scenario where you possess all the skills you ever wished for will give you the strength to act like you already possess those skills. I used to struggle a lot in expressing myself. I was quite shy and was never assertive. In fact, I was quite a pushover. One of my friends always seemed super comfortable with herself and used to radiate self-confidence. I wanted to be more like her. So, what did I do? I started to think and act as she would. I am not suggesting that you must copy someone else and change your behavior. No, this is not what I am suggesting. Instead, I want you to start cultivating such behaviors that are good for you while staying true to your personality and characteristics. Learning to be assertive was something I desired, and by incorporating her behaviors, I realized that I was becoming more assertive. This simple exercise worked really well for me. I didn't change myself. Instead, I became a more confident version of the person I was.

Chapter 8: Inspiring HSPs And Empaths Who Have Achieved Greatness

In this section, let us look at some inspiring real-life empaths who managed to achieve great things in life. A small disclaimer before you start reading this chapter, keep in mind that these are my personal opinions. You don't necessarily have to agree with all that is mentioned herein, but I strongly feel that the empathic abilities of all those discussed in this section are the reason why they achieve the kind of greatness they did.

One of the greatest empaths that ever lived is Mahatma Gandhi. Did you know that Mahatma was a title bestowed upon him by his followers? Mahatma literally means a great soul. Once Gandhi returned to India in 1915, he made up his mind that he was going to start campaigning for Indian independence from the oppressive British rule. Before he could do this, he decided that he needed to experience what life was clearly like for the poorest of power in India. He traded his fancy clothes and donned the humble dhoti (loincloth). He retreated to the quiet life in Sabarmati ashram between the years 1917 to 1930. He lived an extremely simple life and believed that by doing this, he could understand how others live in the country. He had his followers started to grow their own food, make their own cloth, and even clean the washrooms on their own. These jobs were often reserved for the Dalits (class of social untouchables). I know the idea of untouchability might be appalling in this day and age, but it did exist, and sadly, it still does in certain remote areas. Anyway, getting back to the story, untouchability was quite prevalent in Indian society, and so was caste discrimination. By doing all this, it triggered Gandhi's empathy instinct. All the communal violence there is between Hindus and Muslims deeply disturbed him. Gandhi, a devout Hindu, couldn't stand all the violence existing around him. I would like to quote one of my favorite quotes by Gandhi- "I am a Muslim! And a Hindu and a Christian and a Jew- and so are all of you." I think these words resonate today the way they did a couple of decades ago. This statement merely goes on to show his empathic nature. He felt for the poor, he lived with them, and he fought to free India.

One empath who was forgotten even by history is Harriet Beecher Stowe. She was an American novelist. The greatest social challenge during her time and age was slavery, along with the brutal treatment that the plantation workers were doled out. In 1852, Uncle Tom's Cabin was published by home. The story created quite a furrow and sold over 4 million copies within a decade. This book gave an up-close and personal account of the true horrors of slavery, and this was one of the factors that helped trigger the rebellion against slavery. She published a story following the death of her

18-month-old son during the cholera epidemic in Cincinnati in the year 1849. This event triggered the empathy in her for all those women whose children were being forcibly sold into slavery at a very young age. Only when she lost her child did she realize the pain that all those mothers were going through when their young ones were ripped away from their arms.

Another famous empath I would like to talk about is George Orwell. During the 1920s, he was posted in Burma as a colonial police officer. During this time, he witnessed the brutality of colonialism and the havoc it was wrecking on the lives of millions of innocent people. Upon witnessing the colonial brutality, he vowed to take action to rectify all this upon reaching Britain. George Orwell's book Down And Out In Paris and London published in 1933, along with all his political reportage, meant that people finally understood about the way the British Society had marginalized communities and nations across the globe.

Well, these were just some of the popular empaths. This list is not exhaustive, and if you look closely, you will realize that there are empaths present everywhere in the world.

Conclusion

Empathy is a superpower that only a few humans possess. Your empathy makes you unique and extremely powerful. Don't think of empathy as a burden, and instead, think of it as a gift. Living in and navigating through all the chaos in this world and become quite overwhelming for highly sensitive individuals. However, the good news is that you can always control the way you lead your life. There are plenty of things you can never control in life. But the one thing you can always control is your mind. By learning to manage your thoughts and controlling your mind, you can lead a happy, stress-free, and fulfilling life.

If you want to regain control of your life and get the kind of life you always desired, then remember that it takes plenty of effort and commitment. You must do this for the sake of your wellbeing. Always keep in mind that you don't owe anyone anything and that you're not indebted to others. In this book, you were given all the information you require to heal and empower yourself as an empath. Once you've identified your empathic abilities, it's time to take corrective measures to heal any areas of life that are bothering too. Spend some time and understand this gift bestowed upon you. Make yourself aware of the fact that your empathy is not a burden. It's a superpower. Then it is time to assess the kind of empath you are. Carefully go through the list of empaths discussed in this book and recognize the category that fits you the best. Start practicing mindful meditation along with all the other exercises discussed in this book to strengthen your energy.

Learn to deal with energy vampires and other toxic people in your lives without becoming an emotional doormat for them. Learn to say no. It is time to protect yourself. You owe this to yourself. Follow the various exercises to make sure that you are leading a professionally and personally satisfying life. Start forming meaningful connections and get rid of toxic people from your life. By learning to be present at the moment and calming your mind, it becomes easier to be an empath. You must first work on healing yourself from within before you try to help others. Remove any blockages of positive energy in your personal energy field. Only then attempt to help anyone you come across. You must start living your life without any anxiety or hesitation. It is time to get rid of any limiting self-imposed beliefs and restrictions and fully embrace the gift of being an empath. It is time that you not just understand, but also reclaim your birthright to lead a happy life. Don't allow this chaotic world to drain you of your energy.

Now, all that's left for you to do is start practicing all the different exercises given in this book. With conscious and consistent effort, patience, and self-compassion, you can thrive in this overwhelming world. Apart from this, it also helps you regain control of your life and reduce the emotional burden on your shoulders.

If you want to learn more about how you can heal your wounds, then I suggest that you refer to my book on "Empath Healing". Finally, if you found this book helpful and want to inspire other people with your story, then please use the review-function on Amazon.

Resources

https://drjudithorloff.com/top-10-traits-of-an-empath/

https://introvertspring.com/6-empath-problems-how-to-cope/

https://blog.usejournal.com/6-superpowers-every-empath-possesses-and-the-3-things-that-hold-us-back-87e4fdf26d68

https://www.learning-mind.com/types-of-empaths/

https://drjudithorloff.com/the-difference-between-empaths-and-highly-sensitive-people/

https://www.psychologytoday.com/intl/blog/the-athletes-way/201310/the-neuroscience-empathy

https://www.payscale.com/career-news/2017/09/10-tips-dealing-toxic-people-work

https://drjudithorloff.com/3-ways-to-create-sacred-space-at-work/

https://www.aconsciousrethink.com/4097/6-relationship-must-dos-for-empaths-and-hsps/

https://www.joinonelove.org/signs-healthy-relationship/

https://www.yourtango.com/2018314308/toxic-relationship-between-empath-and-narcissist-attraction

https://www.romankrznaric.com/outrospection/2010/03/27/407

http://powerfulmind.co/protect-yourself-from-a-narcissist/

https://introvertspring.com/friendships-tough-highly-sensitive-people/

https://www.prevention.com/health/mental-health/a24748537/signs-narcissistic-parent/

9 783907 269473